# Nelson Comprehension

## Pupil Book

### Yellow

Sarah Lindsay
Series Editor: John Jackman

Nelson Thornes

G000293511

Published in 2009 by:
Nelson Thornes Ltd
Delta Place
27 Bath Road
CHELTENHAM
GL53 6TH
United Kingdom

13 / 10 9 8 7 6 5

A catalogue record for this book is available from the British Library

ISBN 978 1 4085 0550 2

Illustrations by: Jim Eldridge, Mike Lacey, Wes Lowe, Matt Ward, Claire Mumford,
Pedro Penizzotto, Mike Phillips (all c/o Beehive Illustration), and Topics.

Photographs courtesy of: Alamy pp30 (top left), 32 (top right); BeWILDerwood p39,
41 (top); Fotolia pp11 (2 images bottom right), 18-19, 30-33, 38, 41; LEGOLAND
Windsor p39 (top) LEGO, the LEGO logo and LEGOLAND are trademarks of the
LEGO Group ©2008 The LEGO Group; Nicholas Yarsley pp10-13.

Cover image: Pedro Penizzotto

Page layout by Topics – The Creative Partnership, Exeter

Printed in China by 1010 Printing International Ltd

## Acknowledgements

The author and publishers wish to thank the following for permission to use copyright material:

[Unit 5 Write] John Foster for 'Leap Like a Leopard' from Doctor Procter and other rhymes by John Foster,
Oxford University Press. Copyright © 1998 John Foster; [Unit 1] HarperCollins Publishers Ltd for extracts
from Bernard Ashley, A Present for Paul (1996) pp. 2-5, 7-10. Text copyright © 1996 Bernard Ashley; [Unit 8]
David Higham Associates on behalf of the Estate of the author for extracts from Roald Dahl, The Magic Finger,
Penguin (1966) pp. 1-7, 9; Macmillan Children's Books for extracts from Brigid Avison, I Wonder Why….My
Tummy Rumbles, [Unit 4 Write] Kingfisher Books (1993) pp. 16-7, 18. Copyright © Kingfisher Publications
PLC 1993; [Unit 6] extracts and illustrations from Julia Donaldson, The Gruffalo, illustrated by Axel Scheffler
(1999) 3-5. Copyright © 1999 Macmillan Publishers Ltd; and Julia Donaldson, Monkey and Puzzle, illustrated
by Axel Scheffler (2000) pp. 3-4, 6-9. Copyright © 2000 Macmillan Publishers Ltd; [Unit 5 Teach] Marian Reiner
on behalf of the author for Eve Merriam, 'Catch a Little Rhyme' from Catch a Little Rhyme by Eve Merriam.
Copyright © 1966 by Eve Merriam, renewed copyright © 1994; [Unit 3 Write] Usborne Publishing Ltd for an
extract from Stephen Cartwright, 'Little Red Riding Hood' from The Usborne Book of Fairy Tales by Stephen
Cartwright (2004). Copyright © 2004 Usborne Publishing Ltd.

Every effort has been made to trace the copyright holders but if any have been inadvertently overlooked the
publishers will be pleased to make the necessary arrangement at the first opportunity.

# Contents

# Scope and sequence

| Unit | Unit name | Unit focus | Text type / genre |
|------|-----------|------------|-------------------|
| 1 | Familiar settings | Exploring stories with familiar settings | Stories with familiar settin |
| 2 | Instructions | Exploring the role of instructions | Instruction texts |
| 3 | Traditional stories | Exploring different versions of a traditional tale | Traditional stories |
| 4 | Explanations | Exploring the language used in explanation texts | Explanation texts |
| 5 | Patterns on the page | Exploring poems that use patterned language | Poetry – patterns on the page |
| 6 | Stories by the same author | Exploring different stories written by the same author | Different stories by the same author |
| 7 | Information texts | Exploring information texts | Information texts |
| 8 | Extended stories | Exploring longer stories | Extended stories by significant authors |
| 9 | Reports | Exploring non-chronological reports | Non-chronological reports |
| 10 | Poetry | Exploring poetry that looks closely at things | Poetry – Really looking |

| Teach/Talk extract | Write extract | Comprehension skills |
| --- | --- | --- |
| A *Present for Paul*<br>Bernard Ashley | A *Present for Paul*<br>Bernard Ashley | Literal<br>Inference<br>Evaluation – prediction /<br>personal experience |
| *Make a magic potion* | *Making butter* | Literal<br>Analysis – text structure<br>Evaluation – personal<br>experience |
| *Little Red Riding Hood* | *Little Red Riding Hood*<br>Stephen Cartwright | Literal<br>Inference<br>Evaluation: opinion |
| *The 'Me' Machine* | *I Wonder Why My Tummy<br>Rumbles*<br>Brigid Avison | Literal<br>Clarification<br>Analysis: language use /<br>text structure |
| *Catch a Little Rhyme*<br>Eve Merriam | *Leap Like a Leopard*<br>John Foster | Literal<br>Analysis: language use /<br>text structure |
| *The Gruffalo*<br>Julia Donaldson | *Monkey Puzzle*<br>Julia Donaldson | Literal<br>Inference<br>Clarification<br>Evaluation: opinion |
| *Cats* | *Pet Cat Facts* | Literal<br>Analysis – text structure |
| *The Magic Finger*<br>Roald Dahl | *The Magic Finger*<br>Roald Dahl | Literal<br>Clarification<br>Inference<br>Evaluation - empathy |
| *Adventure World* | *Planning a day out* | Literal<br>Summarising<br>Inference |
| *I Wonder*<br>Jeannie Kirby | *Ice Lolly*<br>Pie Corbett | Literal<br>Inference<br>Analysis: language use<br>Evaluation: personal<br>experience |

## Going to the market

It was Saturday and baby Paul was hurting badly with a new tooth coming through.

Pleasure's dad said he'd do the shopping alone – unless his big girl wanted to help.

'But you'd better stay close,' he told her.

'That market's a busy old place today.'

… Going to market Pleasure showed what she'd got in her hand.

'A pound for a present for Paul,' she said. But her Dad was busy checking his list.

… It was all bustle and bags when they got off the bus. And Dad with all that shopping to do.

'Vegetables,' he said, holding her tightly.

And he bought chillies, potatoes and beans.

But Pleasure was eyeing the children's stall.

'I want to get something for Paul.'…

And her hand went straight to her pocket when her father let go to pay. Because over there was a teething ring – just right for the baby to bite.

*A Present for Paul,* Bernard Ashley

- What day of the week is it?
- Where were Pleasure and her dad going?
- How did Pleasure and her dad travel?
- Which vegetables did Dad need to buy?

- How many characters are in this story?
- Who is the main character?
- What is Pleasure like?
- What does she want to do?

- This is the beginning of the story.
  What do you think might happen next?

7

## Where's Dad?

…She was thinking how pleased the baby would be – but the smile was wiped off in a flash.

'Dad…!'

Because her dad wasn't there any more!

*He wasn't there?*

Where was he?

She'd only just turned round, how could he have gone so quick? She twisted back the other way – but he wasn't there either, only strangers' legs and their coats and their bags.

There was everyone else, but no sign of him!

Her stomach did a head over heels – but he always said she was a big girl, so she wasn't going to get scared!

*A Present for Paul*, Bernard Ashley

Copy the right answers.

**1** Who is Pleasure thinking about?
- Pleasure is thinking about her baby brother Paul.
- Pleasure is thinking about her mum.

**2** Why did Pleasure suddenly feel worried?
- Pleasure had lost her money.
- Pleasure had lost her dad.

**3** What did Pleasure's dad always call her?
- He called her his big girl.
- He called her his small girl.

 **4** Have you ever been lost?
How do you think Pleasure feels?
Copy the words that tell us how Pleasure might be feeling.

happy    sad    worried    pleased

scared    bright    upset    frightened

jolly    tearful

 **5** Write a sentence saying how you think the story might end.

9

## Make a magic potion!
*You will need:*

washing-up liquid

a glass jar

clear vinegar

glitter

food dye

bicarbonate of soda    a teaspoon

### What to do:

1   Half fill the jar with the vinegar.

2   Add a teaspoon of food dye and a teaspoon of glitter.

3   Add a big squeeze of washing-up liquid, then stir carefully.

4   Add a heaped teaspoon of bicarbonate of soda.

5   Watch what happens!

**Warning!**
This is **NOT** a drink.

Look at the instructions.

- What do you have to do first?
- What do you add at the same time as the glitter?
- How much washing-up liquid do you add?
- What does the last instruction ask you to do?

Look at how the instructions are written.

- In what order do you find these?

Warning    You will need    Title    What to do

- What different things do we need instructions for?

11

# Making butter

## *You will need:*

some kitchen towels     a clean jar with a lid

a bowl

a sieve     500 ml of cream or fresh full fat milk

## *What to do:*

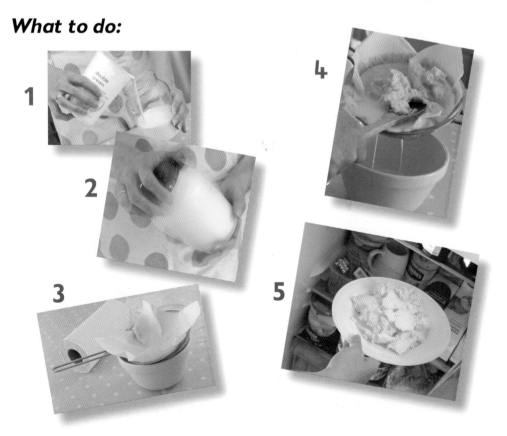

1

2

3

4

5

**1** Write out the instructions in the correct order.

- Shake the jar for 20 minutes (or more), until you have big lumps in the cream.

- Pour the cream into the jar and screw on the lid.

- Pour the contents from the jar into the sieve. The lumps are butter!

- Put the kitchen towel in the sieve and place it over the bowl.

- Put the butter in the fridge. You can eat it when it is cold.

 Answer these questions with a sentence.
**2** How much cream do you need?
**3** When do you stop shaking the cream?
**4** When can you eat the butter?

 **5** How do you make a jam sandwich?
Write your own instructions.

## Little Red Riding Hood

Ruby loved the red hooded top her Granny gave her. She wore it everywhere. Soon people started to call her Little Red Riding Hood.

One morning, Little Red Riding Hood's mum was making cakes in the kitchen. Little Red Riding Hood had an idea.

'Mum,' she said, 'could I take some of your cakes and a drink to Granny? I'm sure she would love them.'

'What a good idea,' her mother said, 'and she'd like to see you too!'

Little Red Riding Hood got her bike ready, put on her helmet and set off.

'Remember, go straight to Granny's and don't talk to strangers,' shouted her mum.

Little Red Riding Hood passed her friends as she rode out of town.

She loved riding to Granny's through the fields, away from the busy roads.

Suddenly, with no warning, a wolf leapt in front of Little Red Riding Hood. She had to brake very quickly.

'Watch out!' she yelled.

The wolf just smiled. 'Show me what is in your basket, little girl. Something smells very nice.'

- Why was the girl called 'Little Red Riding Hood'?

- What was Little Red Riding Hood taking to her granny?

- Where did Little Red Riding Hood meet the wolf?

- What did the wolf want?

- Is Little Red Riding Hood a 'good' or 'bad' character in the story? Why?

- Is the wolf a 'good' or 'bad' character in the story? Why?

15

# Little Red Riding Hood

Little Red Riding Hood and her mother live near a big, dark forest.

Her name comes from a bright red cloak with a hood that her Granny made her.

'Please take this food to your Granny. She's unwell in bed,' says her mother. 'Go through the forest but don't talk to any strangers you meet on the way.'

Little Red Riding Hood waves goodbye.

She walks into the forest with her basket. She doesn't see the Big Black Wolf watching her from behind a tree.

Suddenly the Wolf is on the path.

'Where are you going?' he asks. 'I'm taking this food to Granny,' says Red Riding Hood, feeling very scared.

*Little Red Riding Hood,* Stephen Cartwright

Copy and finish the sentences.

**1** Granny made Little Red Riding Hood's _____.

basket      cloak      cake

**2** Little Red Riding Hood's granny felt _____.

unwell      happy      tired

**3** Little Red Riding Hood walked through
the _____.

field      village      forest

**4** Little Red Riding Hood was scared
of the _____.

forest      wolf      dark

 **5** You have now read the start of
two Little Red Riding Hood stories.

- List what is **different** about the
  two stories.
- List what is the **same** about the
  two stories.

 **6** Which story do you prefer?
Write a sentence to say why.

17

## 📖 Finding information

Index

| B | | |
|---|---|---|
| blinking | 18 | |
| bones | 4, 8–q | |
| brain | 4, 7, 20–21 | |
| burping | 25 | |

| C | | |
|---|---|---|
| cramp | 13 | |

| D | | |
|---|---|---|
| dreaming | 27 | |

| E | | |
|---|---|---|
| ears | 6, 12 | |

| H | | |
|---|---|---|
| hair | 5, 10 | |
| heart | 4, 16–17 | |
| hiccups | 25 | |

| M | | |
|---|---|---|
| mouth | 22 | |

| N | | |
|---|---|---|
| nose | 22 | |

| S | | |
|---|---|---|
| skin | 4, 24 | |
| sleeping | 21, 27 | |

| T | | |
|---|---|---|
| tears | 18 | |
| teeth | 22 | |

| W | | |
|---|---|---|
| windpipe | 14, 15 | |

The 'Me' Machine

Dawn Doneathy

Look at the front cover.

- What is the book about?

- Who wrote the book?

Look at the index.

- What is an index used for?

- On what pages would you find information on the heart?

- On what page would you find information on teeth?

- Blinking can be found on page 18. What else can be found on page 18?

- Dreaming and sleeping can be both found on page 27. Why do you think this is?

# What does my heart do?

heart

Your heart is a very special muscle which keeps blood moving around your body. If you put your hand on your chest near your heart, you'll feel it beating. Each time it beats, it pumps blood out around your body.

To hear a heart beating, find somewhere quiet and rest your ear against a friend's chest. You should hear two sounds close together – 'lub-dub', 'lub-dub', 'lub-dub'.

### How big is my heart?
Our hearts grow with us – they get bigger as we do.
   Whatever size you are now, your heart will be a bit bigger than your fist.

*I Wonder Why My Tummy Rumbles*, Brigid Avison

Copy and finish the sentences.

**1** The heart is a _____.
bone       muscle

**2** The heart pumps _____ around your body.
water       blood

**3** The heart makes _____ sounds close together.
two       four

**4** Your heart is a bit _____ than your fist.
bigger       smaller

 **5** A glossary is a list of special words and their explanations. It is written in alphabetical order.

**a** Choose five words from the page that could go in a glossary.

**b** Write the words you have chosen in alphabetical order.

**c** Add a definition for each word.

a b c d e f g h i j k l m n o p q r s t u v w x y z

**heart:** a muscle that pumps blood around a body

## Catch a Little Rhyme

Once upon a time
I caught a little rhyme

I set it on the floor
but it ran right out the door

I chased it on my bicycle
but it melted to an icicle

I scooped it up in my hat
but it turned into a cat

I caught it by the tail
but it stretched into a whale

I followed it in a boat
but it changed into a goat

When I fed it tin and paper
it became a tall skyscraper

Then it grew into a kite
and flew far out of sight ...

*Catch a Little Rhyme,* Eve Merriam

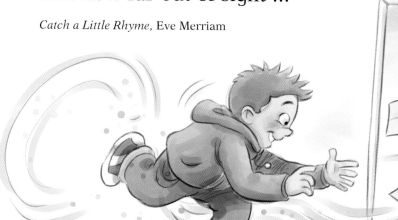

- When the rhyme was put on the floor where did it run?

- Where was the rhyme when it turned into a cat?

- What did the rhyme stretch into?

- What had the rhyme been fed when it became a skyscraper?

- Some of the words in the poem **rhyme**. Find the words that each of these words rhyme with.

boat     time     bicycle     floor     kite     tail

Read the poem again.

- Do you like it?

- Does it make you smile?

- Why?

# Leap Like a Leopard

Leap like a leopard.
Hop like a kangaroo.
Swing from branch to branch
Like a monkey in a zoo.

Dive like a dolphin.
Plunge like a whale.
Creep like a caterpillar.
Crawl like a snail.

Scuttle like a spider.
Slither like a snake.
Slide like a duck
On a frozen lake.

Skip like a lamb.
Jump like a frog.
Stalk like a cat.
Scamper like a dog.

*Leap Like a Leopard*, John Foster

Copy the right answers.

**1** What does the kangaroo do?

- The kangaroo leaps.
- The kangaroo hops.

**2** Where does the monkey swing?

- The monkey swings in a zoo.
- The monkey swings at the playground.

**3** What slides on a frozen lake?

- A snake slides.
- A duck slides.

**4** What does the cat do?

- The cat walks.
- The cat stalks.

 **5** Look at the poem.

- Which word rhymes with 'kangaroo'?
- Which word rhymes with 'whale'?
- Which word rhymes with 'snake'?
- Which word rhymes with 'frog'?

 **6** Look carefully at the poem.

- Write what the poem is about.
- Write the words the poet has repeated.

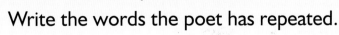

## Silly Old Fox

A mouse took a stroll through the deep dark wood.
A fox saw the mouse and the mouse looked good.

*'Where are you going to, little brown mouse?*
*Come and have lunch in my underground house.'*

'It's terribly kind of you, Fox, but no –
I'm going to have lunch with a gruffalo.'

*'A gruffalo? What's a gruffalo?'*

'A gruffalo! Why, didn't you know?
He has terrible tusks, and terrible claws,
And terrible teeth in his terrible jaws.'

*'Where are you meeting him?'*

'Here, by these rocks,
And his favourite food is roasted fox.'

*'Roasted fox! I'm off!'* Fox said.
*'Goodbye, little mouse,'* and away he sped.

'Silly old Fox! Doesn't he know,
There's no such thing as a gruffalo?'

*The Gruffalo*, Julia Donaldson

- Where is the mouse walking?

- Who does the mouse meet?

- Where does Fox want the mouse to go?

- What does the gruffalo look like?

- Which of these words could be used to describe the mouse? Why?

| | | |
|---|---|---|
| clever | sad | brave |
| timid | brown | frightened |

- Can you think of any more words to describe the mouse?

- What do you like about the story?

- What don't you like about the story?

27

# Come, Little Monkey

'I've lost my mum!'

*'Hush, little monkey, don't you cry.*
*I'll help you find her,' said Butterfly.*
*'Let's have a think. How big is she?'*

'She's big!' said the monkey. 'Bigger than me.'

*'Bigger than you? Then I've seen your mum.*
*Come, little monkey, come, come, come.'*

'No, no, no! That's an elephant.
My mum isn't a great grey hunk.
She hasn't got tusks or a curly trunk.
She doesn't have great thick baggy knees.
And anyway, *her* tail coils round trees.'

*'She coils round trees? Then she's very near.*
*Quick, little monkey! She's over here.'*

'No, no, no! That's a snake.
Mum doesn't look a *bit* like this.
She doesn't slither about and hiss.
She doesn't curl round a nest of eggs.
And anyway, my mum's got more legs.'

*'It's legs we're looking for now, you say?*
*I know where she is, then. Come this way.'…*

*Monkey Puzzle,* Julia Donaldson

Copy the right answers.

**1** Who has the monkey lost?

- The monkey has lost his mum.
- The monkey has lost his home.

**2** Who helped the monkey?

- The elephant helped the monkey.
- The butterfly helped the monkey.

**3** Who has baggy knees?

- The elephant has baggy knees.
- The monkey's mum has baggy knees.

**4** Does the monkey's mum have a nest of eggs?

- No, the monkey's mum doesn't have a nest of eggs.
- Yes, the monkey's mum does have a nest of eggs.

**5** *The Gruffalo* and *Monkey Puzzle* are written by the same author, Julia Donaldson.

- Write a list of the things that are similar in both stories.
- Write a list of the things that are different in both stories.

**6** Which story did you like more?

 *The Gruffalo*       *Monkey Puzzle*

Write a sentence saying why.

## Cats

- There are many different kinds of cat.
- Did you know the big wild cats are related to the cats that live in our homes?
- All cats eat meat.
- Cats have good eyesight and a good sense of smell.

### Pet cats

These cats live with people. They don't have to hunt for their food, but sometimes they catch birds or mice.

### Lions

These cats live in groups called 'prides'. The male lions often relax while the lionesses do most of the hunting.

### Tigers

These are the biggest cats. They like water, which most other cats don't like. They are good swimmers and often relax in the water to cool down.

### Cheetahs

These are the fastest cats. The cheetah is the fastest-running animal in the world.

- Are wild cats related to pet cats?

- What do tigers sometimes do to cool down?

- Which are the biggest cats?

- What do all cats eat?

Look at the sections. In which section do we read about:

- the male cat relaxing

- the cats not having to hunt for food

- the cats enjoying swimming

- the fastest cats?

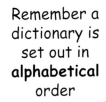

Remember a dictionary is set out in **alphabetical** order

- Look up each of these words in a dictionary.

  pride    relax      tiger

- Do any of the words have more than one meaning?

# Pet cat facts

Cats sometimes eat grass. This can help them cough up fur balls.

Most cats like being brushed.

Cats need to scratch to exercise their muscles.

Cats wash themselves for many hours every day.

If cats miaow when you are near, it can mean they want your attention.

Most cats give birth to four to six kittens, though sometimes they may have as many as twelve.

Cats usually purr when they are happy.

Cats and dogs can be best friends.

Kittens play with moving things. While they are playing they are learning to hunt.

Copy and finish the sentences.

**1** Every day a cat will wash itself for _____.
minutes     hours

**2** A cat may _____ if it is happy.
purr     miaow

**3** Some cats can have as many as _____ kittens.
six     twelve

**4** Sometimes cats eat _____.
grass     fur balls

Don't forget to use capital letters and full stops!

Answer each question with a sentence.

**5** Why do cats scratch?

**6** Do cats like being brushed?

**7** What do kittens learn while they are playing?

Look at the information on 'Cats' on page 30.

Look at the information on 'Pet cat facts' on page 32.

**8** Which information is set out in the most helpful way?
Write a sentence. Don't forget to say why.

## The Magic Finger

*An eight-year-old girl is a friend of the Gregg family …*

Last week, something very funny happened to the Gregg family. I am going to tell you about it as best I can.

Now the one thing that Mr Gregg and his two boys loved to do more than anything else was to go hunting. Every Saturday morning they would take their guns and go off into the woods to look for animals and birds to shoot. Even Philip, who was only eight years old, had a gun of his own.

I can't stand hunting. I just can't *stand* it. It doesn't seem right to me that men and boys should kill animals just for the fun they get out of it. So I used to try to stop Philip and William from doing it …

Then, one Saturday morning, I saw Philip and William coming out of the woods with their father, and they were carrying a lovely young deer.

This made me so cross that I started shouting at them.

The boys laughed and made faces at me, and Mr Gregg told me to go home and mind my own Ps and Qs.

Well, that did it!

I saw red.

And before I was able to stop myself, I did something I never meant to do.

I PUT THE MAGIC FINGER ON THEM ALL!

*The Magic Finger,* Roald Dahl

- What do Mr Gregg and the boys enjoy doing?
- On which day of the week do they go into the woods?
- How old is Philip?
- What made the girl very cross?
- What did the girl do to the Gregg family?

Read the extract again.
- Add three more notes to say what has happened in the story so far.

Mr Gregg and the boys go hunting on Saturday.

They kill a deer.

- Are you enjoying the story so far?

- Is there a line that makes you want to read more of the story?

# The Magic Finger *(continued)*

For months I had been telling myself that I would never put the Magic Finger upon anyone again – not after what happened to my teacher, old Mrs Winter.

Poor old Mrs Winter.

One day we were in class, and she was teaching us spelling. 'Stand up,' she said to me, 'and spell cat.'

'That's an easy one,' I said. 'K-a-t.'

'You are a stupid little girl!' Mrs Winter said.

'I am not a stupid little girl!' I cried. 'I am a very nice little girl!'

'Go and stand in the corner,' Mrs Winter said.

Then I got cross, and I saw red, and I put the Magic Finger on Mrs Winter good and strong, and almost at once …

Guess what?

*Whiskers* began growing out of her face! They were long black whiskers, just like the ones you see on a cat, only much bigger. And how fast they grew! …

Of course the whole class started screaming with laughter …

And when she turned around to write something on the blackboard we saw that she had grown a *tail* as well! It was a huge bushy tail!

I cannot begin to tell you what happened after that, but if any of you are wondering whether Mrs Winter is quite all right again now, the answer is No. And she never will be.

… Well, the Magic Finger was now upon the whole of the Gregg family, and there was no taking it off again.

*The Magic Finger,* Roald Dahl

Copy and finish the sentences.

**1** Mrs Winter was teaching _____.

writing        spelling

**2** _____ had the Magic Finger put on her.

Mrs Winter     A cat

**3** _____ grew out of Mrs Winter's face.

A tail         Whiskers

**4** The whole class started _____.

laughing       crying

**5** Read this section from the story again.

… 'Stand up,' she said to me, 'and spell cat.'
  'That's an easy one,' I said. 'K-a-t.'
  'You are a stupid little girl!' Mrs Winter said.
  'I am not a stupid little girl!' I cried. 'I am a very nice little girl!'

- Write three things this tells us about the girl.

**6** Write what you think happens next to Mr Gregg, Philip and William.

# Adventure World

**Come and discover our fantastic, fun, full-sized pirate ship with soft play island …**

 **Terrific Trampolining**

 **Sinking Sandpit**

 **Swingboats**

 **Tall Tree Houses**

*'Hours of fun, spend the day.'*

*'Loved by children of all ages.'*

*'One of the best adventure playgrounds ever!'*

**Open daily 10am to 4pm**
*(except Christmas Day)*

> I was Captain Tuhil for the day. My friends and I had great fun capturing the island and making my brother walk the plank! I wish we could come back tomorrow.

**Cost:**
**Children £5.00**
**Adults £8.00**

> Child-friendly café for tasty sandwiches, yummy fruit bowl, loads of sweets and delicious drinks.

Sorry, no dogs.
Children must be under 11 years
and accompanied by an adult.

- What is this leaflet about?
- How much is a child's ticket for the day?
- What can children do at the playground?
- Do you need to bring a packed lunch?

Look at Tuhil's comment.
- Did Tuhil enjoy the day?
- What did Tuhil play on?
- Why do you think Tuhil's comment has been included in the leaflet?

Your family are deciding whether to go to the playground.
- What does each bit of information tell you?
- Are they all important?

**Description**     This tells you what you could visit.

**Opening times**    This tells you …
**Cost**    This tells you …
**at people say**    This tells you …

Come to Adventure World!

# Planning a day out

## Where shall we go?

There are many exciting places to visit.
Some are linked with history, such as
castles and old houses.
Others are all about having fun, such
as adventure playgrounds
and seaside piers.

## How much will it cost?

Find out how much the day will cost.
Sometimes it is cheaper to buy a
family ticket instead of single tickets
for each person.
How much will it cost to get there?
Are there things to buy once you
are there?

## How do we get there?

Spend time looking up how to get to
where you want to go.
It might save time on the day!
Often the website of the place will
have a map.

## What shall we take?

Think about the clothes you wear.
Are they comfortable? Will they
keep you dry if it rains?
Do you need to take a packed
lunch?
If it is a long day out, take some
snacks.
Remember to take some money.

Copy and finish the sentences.

**1** There are many _____ places to visit.
exciting       dull

**2** Sometimes it is cheaper to buy a _____ ticket.
family       single

**3** _____ often have a map to show
how to get to a place.
Tickets       Websites

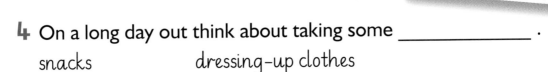

**4** On a long day out think about taking some _____ .
snacks       dressing-up clothes

Answer each question with a sentence.

**5** Which days out are all about having fun?

**6** Why is it important to look up where you are going
before you leave?

**7** How would you choose what clothes to wear
on a day out?

Look at the 'What shall we take?' section.

You could use
bullet points.

**8** Write in note form what you
need to take, like this:

• snacks
• trainers
•
•

41

# I Wonder

I wonder why the grass is green,
And why the wind is never seen?

Who taught the birds to build a nest,
And told the trees to take a rest?

Or, when the moon is not quite round,
Where can the missing bit be found?

Who lights the stars, when they blow out,
And makes the lightning flash about?

Who paints the rainbow in the sky,
And hangs the fluffy clouds so high?

Why is it now, do you suppose,
That Dad won't tell me, if he knows?

*I Wonder*, Jeannie Kirby

What does the poet wonder?

- Why is the grass …?
- Why is the moon …?
- Who lights the …?
- Who paints the …?
- Do you think Dad knows the answers?

 • Find a word in the poem that rhymes with:

nest       green       round
suppose       sky       out

 Listen to the poem again.

- Do you like this poem? Why?
- Do you have a favourite line?

43

# Ice Lolly

Red rocket
on a stick.
If it shines,
lick it quick.

Round the edges,
on the top,
round the bottom,
do not stop.
Suck the lolly,
lick your lips.

Lick the sides
as it drips
off the stick –
quick, quick,
lick, lick –
Red rocket
on a stick.

*Ice Lolly*, Pie Corbett

 Copy the right answers.

**1** What is a 'red rocket'?

- A red rocket is a lolly.
- A red rocket is a stick.

*lick*

**2** Which part of the body does the poem say to lick?

- The poem says to lick your hand.
- The poem says to lick your lips.

*red*

 Write your answers as sentences.

**3** How many times can you find 'lick' written in the poem?

*drips*

**4** Where does the poem say to lick the lolly? (There is more than one answer.)

*suck*

**5** Which other words rhyme with 'lick'?

*lolly*

Remember to write your answers as sentences.

 The poem says 'If it shines, lick it quick'.

**6** Why do you think it says this?

*lips*

**7** What else would you have to eat quickly in the sun?

*rocket*

# How to use this book

*This Pupil Book consists of ten units that help to teach comprehension skills for a range of different text types and genres, including fiction, non-fiction and poetry. It can be used as part of the Nelson Comprehension series, which includes Teacher's Resource Books and CD-ROMs. Each Nelson Comprehension unit is split into three sections.*

**Teach**

The 'Teach' section includes an illustrated text or a picture stimulus for a teacher and children to read together and discuss in class. Extended texts and discussion points are supplied in the accompanying *Teacher's Resource Book*, with full multi-modal whiteboard support (complete with voiceovers and a range of audio and visual features) on the CD-ROM.

**Talk**

The aim of this section is to get the children in small groups to practise the skills they have just learnt. Each child could take on a role within the group, such as scribe, reader or advocate. They are presented with a range of questions to practise the skills they have been learning in the 'Teach' section.

The questions are followed up by a discussion, drama, role play or other group activity to further reinforce their learning. Further guidance is supplied in the *Teacher's Resource Book*, while interactive group activities to support some of the 'Talk' questions and activities are supplied on the CD-ROM.

**Write**

The third section offers an opportunity to test what the children have learnt by providing a new text extract and a series of questions, which can be answered orally, as a class exercise, or as an individual written exercise. The questions include initial literal questions, followed by vocabulary clarification, inference and evaluation questions and then extended follow-up activities. Full answer guidance and PCMs are supplied in the accompanying *Teacher's Resource Book*, while a whiteboard questioning reviewing feature is supplied on the CD-ROM.

# Using the Pupil Book alongside the Nelson Comprehension ICT

*The Nelson Comprehension Pupil Book and Teacher's Resource Book for Yellow level are supported by the Yellow level CD-ROM which provides fully interactive whole-class whiteboard and group computer activities. The CD-ROM includes each of the units and its extracts and texts, and matches the Teach–Talk–Write structure of the Pupil Book.*

**Teach**

The ICT Teach section supplies the Pupil Book / Teacher's Resource Book extract in a multi-media form – with voiceover, sound effects, images and, in some cases, video or animation. The images and voiceover can be switched on and off in order to increase or remove supports for a child's comprehension. A selection of the questions from the Pupil Book is supplied with the ICT, along with the highlighting of clues in the text, a free-type box for scribing possible answers, and model answers to support the modelling of inferring or deducing an answer. A range of annotation tools is also provided so any new questions or points which the teacher or pupil raise can also be highlighted.

*Teach section, Unit 3, CD-Rom, Yellow*

unit 3 | Traditional stories — teach | unit menu

**Little Red Riding Hood**

1 2 3 4 5

Why was the girl called Little Red Riding Hood?

show clues A

Ruby loved the hooded top her Granny gave her. She wore it everywhere. Soon people started to call her Little Red Riding Hood.

## Talk

The ICT Talk section supplements the Pupil Book small group discussion and role-play questions by providing a range of 'Talk activities'. These ICT activities are specially designed to stimulate discussion or support a drama activity in relation to a particular comprehension question. The ICT

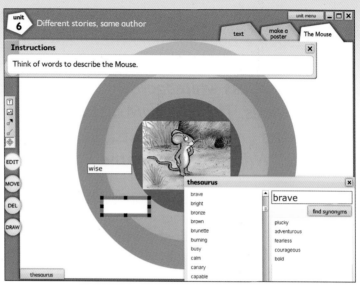

activities include: dilemma vote, character grid, story map, information categoriser, sequencer, question maker and a text formatter (which allows children to create their own playscript or other specific text type).

## Write

The ICT Write section is designed to provide a whiteboard or desktop reviewing system for children who have completed or are engaged in a class or group discussion of the Write extract and activities in the Pupil Book. As in the Teach section, all the questions are provided, along with

selectable clue highlights, a free-type facility and a model answer which gives an idea of a plausible answer to the question. All questions can be hovered over with the mouse to reveal a definition of the type of comprehension question it is.

# energy

## 1

## Steve Elsworth
## Jim Rose

PEARSON
Longman

ⓒⓒ  = Cross curricular materials

ⓟ  = For your portfolio

📼 = Listen to the text on the class cassette too

2

| Communication | Skills | Memory Gym | Writing Gym |
|---|---|---|---|
| Ask about names<br>Give personal details | **Reading:** About the band<br>**Listening:** The pop charts | | |
| Start a conversation<br>Ask personal questions | **Reading:** Different text types<br>**Listening:** Mel and Isabel meet<br>**Study skills:** Reading – text types | 1 Countries and nationalities | 1 An e-mail ⓟ<br>**Writing Tip:**<br>Capital letters |
| Describe things and places<br>Describe your bedroom | **Reading:** 1) Letter from Samoa ⓒⓒ ▸▭•<br>2) A room in the Antarctic ▸▭•<br>**Listening:** Isabel plans her bedroom<br>**Study skills:** Reading – prediction | 2 Everyday things<br>3 Furniture and prepositions | 2 A letter about your room ⓟ<br>**Writing Tip:**<br>Using adjectives |
| Polite requests<br>Describe families and people<br>**Pronunciation:** /θ/, /ð/ | **Reading:** 1) Mickey's family ▭•<br>2) The Star Wars family<br>**Listening:** Descriptions of 5 people<br>**Study skills:** Writing – write a draft | 4 Personality adjectives<br>5 Appearances<br>6 Families | 3 A description of a person ⓟ<br>**Writing Tip:** Linkers *and/but* |
| Ask about times<br>Talk about daily routines<br>Phone the cinema | **Reading:** 1) *Buffy* ▸▭•<br>2) The Original Chewing Gum ⓒⓒ ▸▭•<br>**Listening:** 3 people talk about their jobs<br>**Study skills:** Listening – get ready to listen | 7 Daily activity verbs | 4 A description of a daily routine ⓟ<br>**Writing Tip:** Linkers *so/ because* |
| Introduce people<br>Ask about free time | **Reading:** 1) A letter from Isabel ▸▭•<br>2) East meets West ⓒⓒ ▸▭•<br>**Listening:** Alan talks about his house<br>**Study skills:** Speaking – get ready | 8 Free time activities<br>9 Rooms | 5 An article about your school ⓟ<br>**Writing Tip:**<br>Punctuation |

ⓒⓒ = Cross curricular materials

ⓟ = For your portfolio

🔊 = Listen to the text on the class cassette too

4

| Communication | Skills | Memory Gym | Writing Gym |
|---|---|---|---|
| Make suggestions<br>Talk about abilities | **Reading:** Can gorillas talk to people? (cc) [cassette]<br>**Listening:** How Koko uses sign language<br>**Study skills:** Reading – look for paragraphs | 10 Adjectives<br>11 Parts of the body | 6 A description of an animal (P)<br>**Writing Tip:** Paragraphs |
| | | | |
| | | | |
| | | | |
| Describe a scene<br>Buy things | **Reading:** Do you want to be a Pop Star? [cassette]<br>**Listening:** An interview with 3 contestants<br>**Study skills:** Dictionary work | 12 Music | 7 A form (P)<br>**Writing Tip:** Addresses and phone numbers |
| | | | |
| | | | |
| Interview a star<br>Talk about the past | **Reading:** 1) My so called life [cassette]<br>2) Meet Aimee Mullins (cc) [cassette]<br>**Listening:** Katie talks about her life<br>**Study skills:** Dictionaries | 13 Dates and months | 8 A webpage (P)<br>**Writing Tip:** Time phrases |
| | | | |
| | | | |
| Offer help<br>Talk about sport<br>**Pronunciation:** /eɪ/, /əʊ/, /aɪ/ | **Reading:** 1) The history of skateboarding (cc) [cassette]<br>2) A profile of David Beckham [cassette]<br>**Listening:** A football training camp<br>**Study skills:** Listening – listening for gist | 14 Sport<br>15 Irregular verbs | 9 A postcard (P)<br>**Writing Tip:** Past simple regular verb spelling |
| | | | |
| | | | |
| | | | |
| Ask permission | **Reading:** 1) What do your clothes say about you? 2) A school review [cassette]<br>**Listening:** descriptions of people<br>**Study skills:** Speaking – conversational replies | 16 Clothes | 10 A review (P)<br>**Writing Tip:** Strong adjectives |
| | | | |
| | | | |
| | | | |
| | | | |

# Meet the band

Isabel Ferrante

**Grammar**

*to be* singular
*Wh-* questions
*a/an* + singular nouns
Plural nouns

**Vocabulary**

Alphabet
Numbers
Colours

**Communication**

Ask about names
Give personal details

## Vocabulary – Alphabet

**1** In pairs, say the letters.

A B C D E F G H
I J K L M N O P
Q R S T U V W
X Y Z

**2** Listen and check your pronunciation.

**3** Listen and write the letters.

*X, I, …*

**4** Say the letters.

DJ OK CD TV DVD www

**5** Read and listen to Isabel and her teacher. Then listen and repeat.

**Teacher** What's your name?
**Isabel** My name's Isabel Ferrante.
**Teacher** How do you spell it?
**Isabel** I-S-A-B-E-L F-E-R-R-A-N-T-E

**6** Interview 5 people. Invent names if you want to.

A: What's your name?
B: My name's … .
A: How do you spell it?
B: … .

**7** Match Isabel's text conversation to the correct phrases.

| 1 | RU OK? | a) Today? |
| 2 | GR8 RU? | b) See you. Love Isabel. |
| 3 | Yes I wan2 CU | c) Great! Are you? |
| 4 | 2day? | d) OK. See you later. |
| 5 | Yes W8 4 me | e) Yes. Wait for me. |
| 6 | Ok CU L8R | f) Yes. I want to see you. |
| 7 | CU Luv I :) | g) Are you OK? |

**Tom Adamski**

## Grammar

> **a/an + singular nouns**
>
> - Use **a** before consonants (b,c,d etc).
>   *a guitar*
> - Use **an** before vowels (a,e,i,o,u).
>   *an apple*

**8** Look at the photo of Tom Adamski above. Make a list of the words you know. Use *a/an*.

*a hamburger*

## Communication – Ask about names

**9** In pairs, ask and answer about the people in the photos below.

| | | |
|---|---|---|
| Robbie Williams | Spiderman | Tiger Woods |
| Beyonce Knowles | Brad Pitt | Jennifer Lopez |

A: What's his/her name?
B: His/Her name's … ./I don't know.

**10** In pairs, ask and answer about the people in your class.

A: What's his/her name?
B: His/Her name's … .

Remember

His 🚶 Her 🚶

## Vocabulary – Numbers

 **1** Listen and repeat the numbers.

| 1 | NEW | Justin Timberlake |
|----|-----|-------------------|
| 2 | | |
| 3 | | |
| 4 | ▼ | The Cheeky Girls |
| 5 | NEW | Radiohead |
| 6 | | |
| 7 | ▲ | Foo Fighters |
| 8 | | |
| 9 | | |
| 10 | ▼ | Madonna |
| 11 | NEW | Christina Aguilera |
| 12 | | |
| 13 | ▲ | Big Brovaz |
| 14 | | |
| 15 | | |
| 16 | ▲ | Shakira |
| 17 | | |
| 18 | ▼ | Eminem |
| 19 | | |
| 20 | ▲ | Sugababes |

## Find out!

**2** Student A look at this page. Student B look at page 134. Complete the chart.

A: What's number three?
B: It's … .
A: How do you spell it?

 **3** Put the numbers into the correct order. Then listen and check.

| ten fifty twenty eighty thirty forty |
|---|
| sixty ninety seventy a hundred |

*ten, …*

 **4** Listen and repeat the numbers.

**a)** 78    **c)** 67    **e)** 45    **g)** 61
**b)** 54    **d)** 21    **f)** 32

**5** Write the numbers in exercise 4 as words.

*a) seventy-eight*

> **Remember**
>
> 200 = two hundred
> 630 = six hundred and thirty
> 5,000 = five thousand
> 8,000,000 = eight million

Mickey Kelly

## Communication – Give personal details

**6** Match the questions to the correct answers. Then listen and check.

1 Mickey, how old are you?
2 How tall are you?
3 What's your favourite number?

a) It's number ten.
b) I'm fourteen.
c) I'm one metre sixty-seven.

**7** In pairs, interview Tom and Isabel. Then ask your partner about himself/herself.

A: Isabel, how old are you?
B: I'm … .

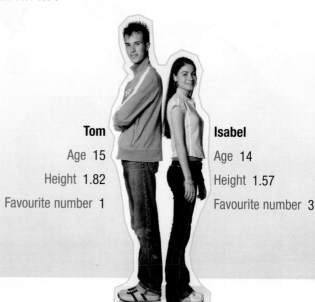

**Tom**
Age 15
Height 1.82
Favourite number 1

**Isabel**
Age 14
Height 1.57
Favourite number 3

## Vocabulary – Colours

**8** Read about Dave. What's his favourite colour?

**9** Match the words to the correct colours.

pink  blue  yellow  green
brown  black  red  white

*1 pink*

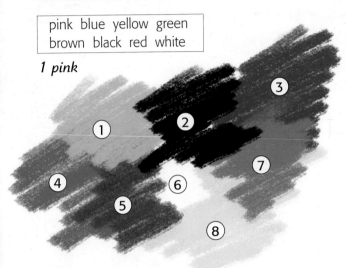

**10** Ask 5 people about their favourite colours.

A: What's your favourite colour?
B: It's … .

## Grammar

| Plural nouns | | | |
|---|---|---|---|
| **Regular nouns** | | **Irregular nouns** | |
| **Singular** | **Plural** | **Singular** | **Plural** |
| drum | drums | person | people |
| eye | eyes | man | men |
| | | woman | women |
| | | child | children |

**Think about language**

**Make rules.**

* To make a plural regular noun add …
* We use/don't use *a/an* with plural nouns.

**11** Make plural nouns.

1  a guitar  *guitars*
2  a man
3  a name
4  a hamburger
5  a person
6  an apple
7  a woman
8  a computer

My name is Dave Black.
My hair is black, my eyes
are black, my room is black
and my drums are black.
My favourite colour is …
BLACK!

Dave Black

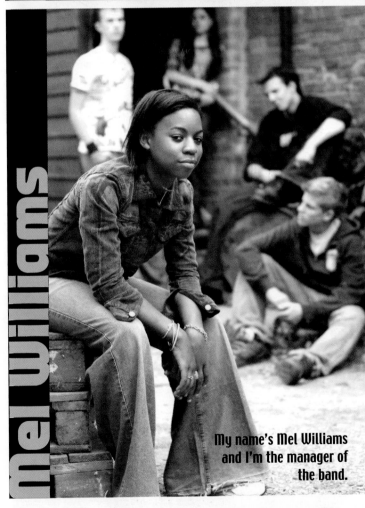

Mel Williams

My name's Mel Williams
and I'm the manager of
the band.

# What's the story of the band?

Turn the page and find out …

# New people

**Grammar**

*to be*
Subject pronouns
Possessive adjectives

**Vocabulary**

Countries and nationalities

**Communication**

Start a conversation
Ask personal questions

FOCUS 1    Switch on

**Listening**

**1** Listen. What are the names of the people in the photo?

## Reading

| | |
|---|---|
| Tom | Who's that? |
| Mel | I don't know. She's a new student. |
| Tom | She's nice. |
| Mel | Tom! |
| Isabel | Excuse me, is this seat free? |
| Tom | Yes, it is. |
| Isabel | Thank you. |
| Mel | You're welcome. What's your name? |
| Isabel | Isabel. |
| Mel | Hi, Isabel. My name's Mel and this is Tom. |
| Isabel | Hello. Nice to meet you. |
| Tom | Where are you from, Isabel? |
| Isabel | I'm from Argentina. And you two? Are you from Manchester? |
| Mel | I am, but Tom isn't. |
| Tom | I'm from Poland. |

**STUDENT PROFILES**

**Name** Tom
**Country** Poland
**Parents** Marek (dad) from Poland
**Other information** student, musician (guitarist)

**Name** Mel
**Country** Britain
**Parents** Esther (mum), Louis (dad) from Trinidad
**Other information** student, writer for the school webpage

**2** Read and complete the sentences.

1 Isabel is a new *student* .
2 Isabel is from … .
3 Mel is from … .
4 Tom isn't from … .
5 Tom's from … .

## Grammar

| Subject pronouns | Possessive adjectives |
|---|---|
| I | my |
| you | your |
| he | his |
| she | her |
| it | its |
| we | our |
| they | their |

**3** Choose the correct words.

1 She/Her is nice.
2 I/My name's Mel.
3 What's he/his name?
4 I/My am from Argentina.
5 We/Our are students.
6 They/Their are from Manchester.
7 You/Your are welcome.
8 A: Is this seat free?
  B: Yes, its/it is.

**4** Read Mel's student profile. Then complete the text about her.

1 *Her* name's Mel. 2 …'s from Britain.
3 …'s a student, and 4 …'s a writer for the school webpage. 5 … parents are from Trinidad.
6 … names are Esther and Louis.

**5** Read Tom's student profile. Then write about him.

*His name's Tom and …*

## Roleplay – Start a conversation

**6** Put the conversation into the correct order.

a) Thank you.
b) Yes, it is.
c) You're welcome. What's your name?
d) Nice to meet you. I'm Jamie.
e) My name's Lisa.
f) Excuse me. Is this seat free? ①

**7** In pairs, imagine you are in a café. Start a conversation.

# FOCUS 2   Grammar – *to be*

| Positive | Negative | Questions | Short answers |
|---|---|---|---|
| I'm (am)<br>you're (are)<br>he's/she's/it's (is)<br>we're/they're (are) | I'm not (am not)<br>you aren't (are not)<br>he/she/it isn't (is not)<br>we/they aren't (are not) | Am I ...?<br>Are you ...?<br>Is he/she/it ...?<br>Are we/they ...? | Yes, I am./No, I'm not.<br>Yes, you are./No, you aren't. |
| | | | ***Wh-* questions** |
| *I'm from Argentina.* | *She isn't from Poland.* | *Are you from Poland?* | *What's his name?*<br>*Where are you from?* |

### Think about language

**Make a rule.**

In questions, the subject
(*I, you*) is <u>before/after</u>
the verb.

*They* are here.
*Are* **they** here?

**1** Read Mel's article about Isabel for the school
webpage. Find the long forms of *to be*.

**2** Complete Mel's article. Use short forms of *to be*.

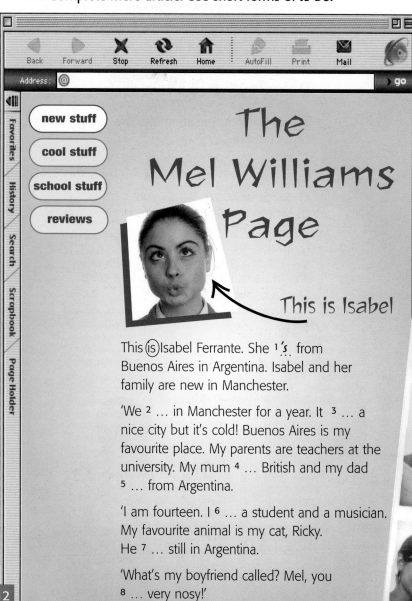

**new stuff**
**cool stuff**
**school stuff**
**reviews**

# The Mel Williams Page

This is Isabel

This (is) Isabel Ferrante. She ¹ 's from
Buenos Aires in Argentina. Isabel and her
family are new in Manchester.

'We ² ... in Manchester for a year. It ³ ... a
nice city but it's cold! Buenos Aires is my
favourite place. My parents are teachers at the
university. My mum ⁴ ... British and my dad
⁵ ... from Argentina.

'I am fourteen. I ⁶ ... a student and a musician.
My favourite animal is my cat, Ricky.
He ⁷ ... still in Argentina.

'What's my boyfriend called? Mel, you
⁸ ... very nosy!'

**3** Make sentences.

1  Isabel/from Argentina

*Isabel's from Argentina.*

2  her dad/from Argentina too
3  her mum/British
4  her parents/teachers
5  Ricky/her cat
6  Manchester/a cold city
7  Isabel and Mel/students
8  we/new in Manchester

**4** Correct the sentences.
Write true sentences.

1  Isabel is from Britain.

*She isn't from Britain.*
*She's from Argentina.*

2  Isabel and her family are in
Buenos Aires for a year.
3  Her favourite place is Manchester.
4  Her parents are students.
5  Her mum is from Argentina.
6  Her dad is from Manchester.
7  Isabel is sixteen.
8  Ricky is in Manchester.

Remember
*to be* short forms
'm = am
's = is
're = are

12

# FOCUS 3   Communication – Ask personal questions

**1** In pairs, answer the questions for Isabel.

**A:** Are you from Manchester?
**B:** No, I'm not. I'm from Buenos Aires.

1 Are you from Manchester?

2 Are you a student?

3 Are your parents students?

4 Is your dad British?

5 Is your mum from Argentina?

6 Are you fifteen?

7 Are you and your family in Manchester for two years?

8 Is Buenos Aires your favourite place?

**2** Match Isabel's questions to Mel's answers. Then listen and check.

| | | | |
|---|---|---|---|
| 1 | What's your name? | a) | She's called Esther. |
| 2 | Where are you from? | b) | Melissa. Call me Mel. |
| 3 | How old are you? | c) | fifteen |
| 4 | What's your father called? | d) | My Manchester United shirt. |
| 5 | What's your mother called? | e) | Manchester |
| 6 | What's your favourite colour? | f) | He's called Louis. |
| 7 | What's your favourite thing? | g) | green |

**3** In pairs, ask and answer the questions in exercise 2 about you.

**A:** What's your name?
**B:** My name's … .

**4** Tell the class about your partner.

*His/Her name is … . He's/She's from … .*

## Find out!

**5** Student A go to page 134. Student B go to page 136. Use questions 2–7 from exercise 2. Who is your partner?

**A:** Where are you from?
**B:** I'm from … .

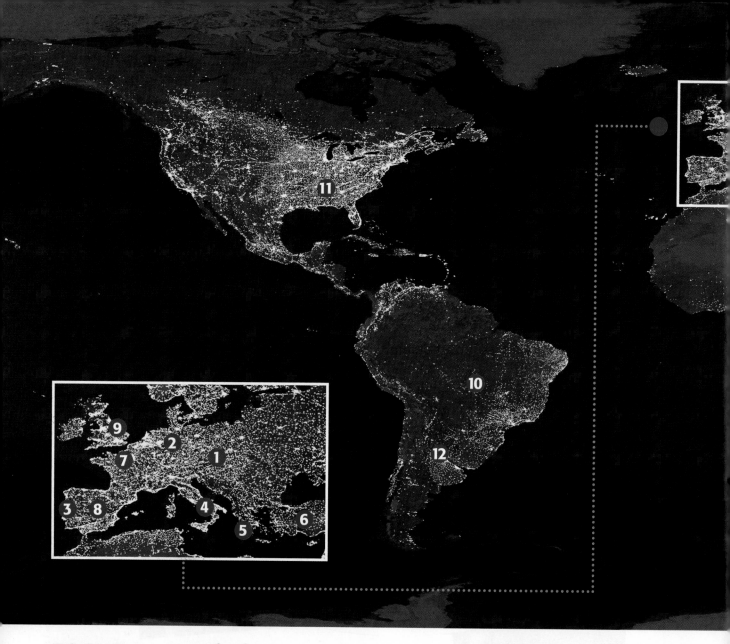

# FOCUS 4  Vocabulary – Countries and nationalities

**1** Make a list of the countries you know in English.

*Japan, …*

**2** In pairs, look at the map. What are the countries? Use the list below to help you.

| | | | |
|---|---|---|---|
| Poland | Brazil | Argentina | Germany |
| Portugal | Russia | Great Britain | Turkey |
| Japan | Greece | Spain | France |
| Australia | Italy | the USA | |

**A:** What's number 1?
**B:** It's Poland.

## Pronunciation – Word stress

**3** Listen and mark the stress on the countries.

Poland  Brazil  Argentina

**4** Match the countries from exercise 2 to the correct nationalities.

| | | | |
|---|---|---|---|
| Polish | Turkish | British | Greek |
| Portuguese | Russian | Italian | Brazilian |
| American | Australian | Argentinian | |
| French | Japanese | German | Spanish |

*Poland – Polish*

**5** Listen and repeat the countries and nationalities.

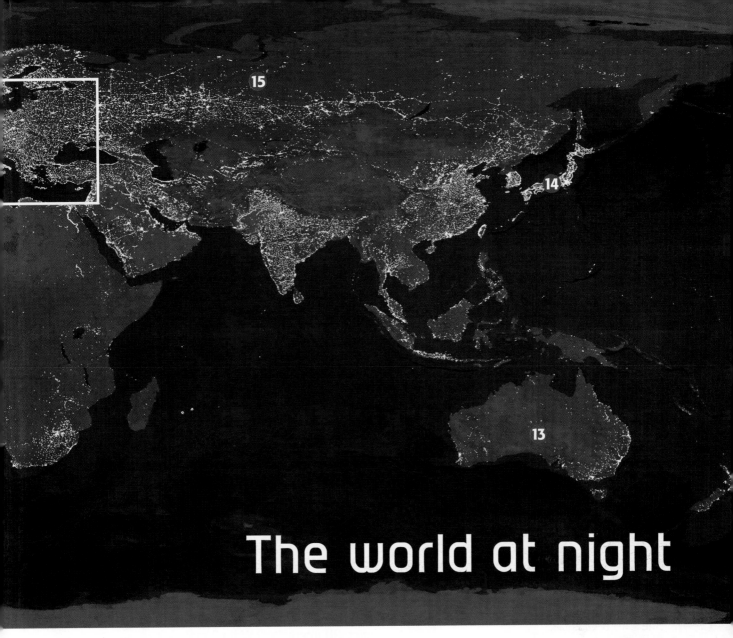

15

14

13

# The world at night

## Memory Tip 1

**Write down new words.**

- Write down new words to help you fix them in your memory.
- Write new words in your Wordstore Book and mark the stress.

Poland
Polish
Brazil
Brazilian

**6** In pairs, ask and answer about the people.

A: Where's Serena Williams from?
B: the USA/I don't know.

*Mel Gibson*

*Michael Schumacher*

*Serena Williams*

*Catherine Zeta-Jones*

**7** In pairs, ask and answer about famous people you know.

## Memory Gym 1

Countries and nationalities

Go to page 116 ▷▷▷

# FOCUS 5 Skills – Write to me

International Student Identity Card
Carte internationale d'étudiant/Carnet internacional de estudiante

a

ISIC
2002
Valid till 30 01 31 Dec 02
T3973733

| Name | Jacek Wysocki |
| Address | Poziomkowa 21 |
| | 23-996 Opole |
| | Poland |
| Date of birth | 30/03/1988 |
| Number | 674045013 |

STUDENT

## Study skills – Reading

**Text types**

There are lots of different types of written texts.
- How many types of text can you think of (in any language)?
- How do the texts look different?
- Before you read a text, look at the pictures and design.

## Reading

**1** Think about the study skill. How many text types can you find in your classroom?

**2** Quick Read. Match the texts to the correct text types.

1  an e-mail *(e)*
2  a letter
3  a postcard
4  an Internet chatroom
5  a speech bubble
6  an identity (ID) card

c

## Teen chat

blah!

:-]

EXIT CHATROOM

**Topic: Internet Buddies**

> **< Popi >** Hi there! How RU? My name's Penelopi Popadopoulos, but my nickname's Popi. I'm from Athens in Greece. I'm fourteen and I wan2 chat. RU interested? Write 2 me! : – )
> **< AJ >** Hi! Popi! How RU?

| 10 Users |
|---|
| **Popi** |
| Peony |
| Susie |
| Bobbie |
| Carrots |
| AJ |
| Tom |
| Jo |
| Emma |
| Jack |

Type your comments in the box.   Then press the ENTER key

**3** Detailed Read. Who are they? Read the texts and find the names.

1  He's from Poland. *Jacek*
2  She's from Valencia.
3  She's from Britain.
4  Her favourite singers are Destiny's Child and Robbie Williams.
5  He's Turkish.
6  She's from Greece.
7  His guitar is his favourite thing.
8  Her favourite place is the beach.

**4** Write the phrases as words.

1  I wan2 chat. *I want to chat.*
2  How RU?
3  Write 2 me.
4  RU interested?

e

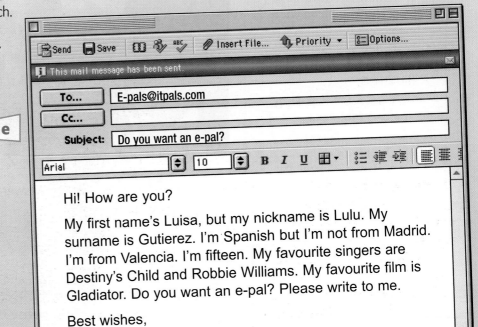

Send  Save  ABC  Insert File...  Priority ▾  Options...

This mail message has been sent.

| To... | E-pals@itpals.com |
| Cc... | |
| Subject: | Do you want an e-pal? |

Arial    10    **B** *I* U

Hi! How are you?

My first name's Luisa, but my nickname is Lulu. My surname is Gutierez. I'm Spanish but I'm not from Madrid. I'm from Valencia. I'm fifteen. My favourite singers are Destiny's Child and Robbie Williams. My favourite film is Gladiator. Do you want an e-pal? Please write to me.

Best wishes,

Lulu

**b**

*My name's Elizabeth – Elizabeth Windsor. I'm from Britain and I'm the Queen!*

**d**

Mutlu Sitesi
18 Blok No 5
Oran
Ankara

Dear Sarah,

My name's Ali. I'm Turkish. I'm from Ankara, the capital of Turkey.
I'm fifteen. My favourite thing is my guitar. Write to me.

Best wishes,

Ali

My guitar is cool!

## Listening

**5** Listen and complete the table about the 2 people.

|  | A | B |
|---|---|---|
| Name | Liz Roberts |  |
| From |  |  |
| Age |  |  |
| Favourite thing |  |  |

## Speaking

**6** In pairs, check your answers to exercise 5. Use the questions from the recording.

A: What's your name?
B: My name's Liz Roberts.

**7** Choose a person from pages 16–17. In pairs, ask and answer to find out who your partner chooses.

A: Where's he or she from?
B: He's from Turkey.

## Writing Gym 1

An e-mail

Go to page 124

**f**

Hi, Katie

Are you my new pen pal?
I'm Maria Paz. I'm sixteen and I'm from Mar del Plata in Argentina.

This is a picture of Mar del Plata at night. The beach is fantastic – it's my favourite place.

Maria

Katie Rose
54 Longwood Road
London
SW7
England

Mar del Plata

17

# Energy Check

## Grammar

**1** Choose the correct words.

1 I/My name's Mel.
2 How old are you/your?
3 She/Her name's Isabel.
4 He/His is Dave Black.
5 His/Her name's Tom.
6 We/Our are Italian.
7 They/Their parents are from Spain.
8 It's/Its a Japanese computer.

**2** Complete the sentences. Use the correct form of *to be*.

1 I *'m* from Poland.
2 She … a new student.
3 We … musicians.
4 It … my ID card.
5 My parents … Spanish.
6 He … my friend.

**3** Put the questions into the correct order.

1 name/your/what's/?

*What's your name?*

2 you/old/are/how/?
3 from/are/where/you/?
4 is/new/student/who/the/?
5 father/'s/called/what/your/?
6 favourite/what/'s/thing/your/?

**4** Correct the sentences. Write true sentences.

1 Paris is in Germany.

*Paris isn't in Germany. It's in France.*

2 George W Bush is Italian.
3 Robbie Williams is from Spain.
4 Hamburgers are from Argentina.
5 Pizza is from Japan.
6 Manchester is in Australia.
7 Jennifer Lopez is British.
8 London is in Russia.

**5** Use *a* or *an* before the words.

1 *an* apple       4 person
2 man            5 eye
3 passport        6 address book

**6** Write the plural forms of the nouns in exercise 5.

1 *apples*

## Vocabulary

**7** Complete with the missing numbers.

1 one, two, *three*.
2 ten, twenty, …
3 five, fifteen, …
4 two hundred, two hundred and fifty, …
5 five hundred, one thousand, …
6 twenty-five, fifty, …

**8** Complete the names of the countries.

| | | |
|---|---|---|
| 1 Brit*ain* | 5 Port … | 9 Gre … |
| 2 Turk … | 6 Braz … | 10 Sp … |
| 3 It … | 7 Pol … | 11 Austral … |
| 4 Germ … | 8 Jap … | 12 Argent … |

**9** Write the nationalities for the countries in exercise 8.

*1 British*

**10** Write the colours.

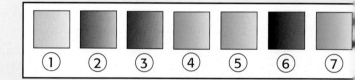

*1 yellow*

## Communication

**11** Complete the conversation.

| | |
|---|---|
| Marco | Excuse me, is this seat free? |
| Anna | Yes, [1] *it is* . |
| Marco | Thank you. |
| Anna | You're [2] … . What's [3] …… ? |
| Marco | Marco. |
| Anna | Hi, Marco. My [4] … Anna. |
| Marco | Hello. Nice to [5] …… . |
| Anna | Where [6] …… ? |
| Marco | [7] …… Italy. |
| Anna | How [8] …… ? |
| Marco | [9] … fifteen. |

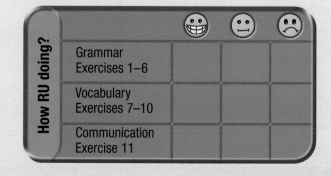

city of Manchester stadium

**1** Hi! I'm fifteen and my name's James. I'm from Manchester – a big city in England. The population is 2.5 million.

**2** Manchester's great, but it's cold. My favourite place in the city is the new City of Manchester Football stadium. I'm a big Manchester City Fan. No, not Man United.

ace = great

**3** My mum isn't from Manchester, she's from Edinburgh, the capital city of Scotland. My friends are from all round Britain. Ellie is from Belfast in Northern Ireland – she's really nice and Jerry is from Wales. He's a surfer. Surfing's ace in Wales! We're all e-pals…and Man City fans. Come on Blues!

## Culture FiLe

|  | Population | Capital |
| --- | --- | --- |
| England | 50 million | London |
| Scotland | 5 million | Edinburgh |
| Wales | 3 million | Cardiff |
| Northern Ireland | 1.7 million | Belfast |

## QUESTIONS

**1** Read about James and answer the questions.

1 What's the population of Manchester?
2 Where is James's favourite place?
3 Where are these people from?
   a) James b) James's mum c) Ellie d) Jerry
4 What is the capital of Northern Ireland?

**2** In groups, discuss the questions.

1 What about your country? What's the capital? What's the population?
2 Where is your favourite place?

19

**Grammar**

Possessive *'s*
*this/that/these/those*
*there is/are*

**Vocabulary**

Everyday things
Furniture
Prepositions of place

**Communication**

Describe things and places
Describe your bedroom

## FOCUS 1    Switch on

### Listening

**1** Check these words.

> band   passport   old   photo

**2** Listen and answer the questions.

1   Where are they?
2   Where is the old photo of Tom?

## Reading

**Mel**     This is Tom's room. Oh, yuk! There's an old pizza on the chair!

**Isabel**  I think this room's great! What's that, Tom?

**Tom**     It's a poster of my band. I'm on the left.

**Isabel**  Really? A band with two people in it?

**Tom**     Yeah, why not?

**Isabel**  Who's that?

**Tom**     My friend, Dave Black.

**Mel**     Dave's crazy.

**Isabel**  What's this Tom?

**Tom**     It's my passport. That's an old photo!

**Isabel**  Is this your real name?

**Tom**     Yes. In English it's Thomas. In Polish it's Tomasz.

**Mel**     Wow! How do you spell it?

**Tom**     I-T

**Mel**     Oh, very funny, Tom.

**Isabel**  What's your dog called?

**Tom**     Merlin.

**Mel**     Hey, Merlin! That's Tom's bag. Look out!

**3** **Read and answer the questions.**

1  Who's in the band?
2  What's Tomasz in English?
3  What's the dog called?

## Grammar

| Possessive *'s* |
| --- |
| *Tom's room.* |
| *Mel's bag.* |

**4** **Make a sentence for the pictures.**

*Number one is Tom's bag.*

**5** **Find and complete the exclamations from the conversation.**

1  Y <u>u k</u> !        4  H _ _ !
2  R _ _ _ _ _ ?        5  L _ _ _  _ _ _ !
3  W _ _ !

**6** **Listen to 4 different situations. Write the correct exclamation for each situation.**

1  *Hey*! That's my bag!        3  … ! It isn't funny!

2  … ! It's a computer!        4  … ! How tall are you?

**7** **Listen again and repeat.**

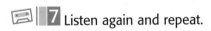
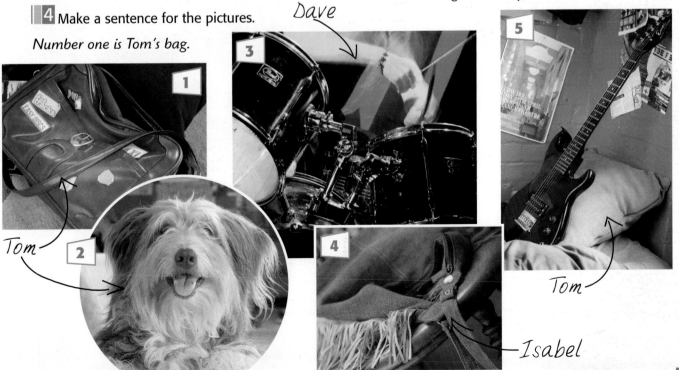

Dave

Tom

Isabel

21

# FOCUS 2  Vocabulary – Everyday things

**1** Match the words to the correct things in the photo.

| | | |
|---|---|---|
| cup *10* | dog | mobile |
| orange | CD | wallet |
| pens | CD player | bottle of cola |
| envelope | cap | guitar |
| ruler | notebook | chocolate bar |
| pencil | camera | passport |
| crisps | keys | |
| ID card | magazines | |

**2** Which words are plural?

*pens, …*

**3** Make the singular words plural.

*dog → dogs*

# FOCUS 3 Grammar – *this/that/these/those*

| Singular | | Plural | |
|---|---|---|---|
| *What's this?* | *What's that?* | *What are these?* | *What are those?* |
|  |  |  |  |

**Think about language**

**Make rules.**

- The plural of **this** is ... .
- The plural of **that** is ... .

**1** Choose the correct words.

1 Are this/these your CDs?
2 What's that/those?
3 These/This aren't your crisps! They're my crisps!
4 Hey! That/Those is my bottle of cola.
5 Are that/those Dave's keys?
6 This/These is my sister.

**2** In pairs, ask and answer about the photo.

A: What's that?
B: It's a cap.
A: What are these?
B: They're CDs.

**3** In pairs, ask and answer about the things in your bag and in your classroom.

A: What's this/that?
B: It's a ... .
A: What are these/those?
B: They're ... .

*Remember*

Don't use a or an with plural nouns.
dogs    guitars

## Pronunciation – /ɪ/, /iː/

**4** Listen and repeat the words.

/ɪ/  th<u>i</u>s  <u>i</u>t  <u>I</u>sabel
/iː/  th<u>e</u>se  thr<u>ee</u>  <u>C</u>Ds

**5** Listen and put the words into the correct columns.

| th<u>i</u>ng | key | maga<u>zi</u>nes | cri<u>s</u>ps | sh<u>e</u> |
|---|---|---|---|---|
| wall<u>e</u>t | guitar | Gr<u>ee</u>k | English | |

| /ɪ/ | /iː/ |
|---|---|
| *thing* | *key* |

## Memory Tip 2

**Remember words in a group or pattern.**

**6** In pairs, put the words on page 22 into groups.

a) Which things are food or drink?
b) Which things are for school?
c) Which things are in your bag?

**Memory Gym 2**

Everyday things

Go to page 116

# FOCUS 4   Grammar – *there is/there are* with plurals

| | Positive | Negative | Questions | Short answers |
|---|---|---|---|---|
| **Singular** | There's (is) a bag. | There isn't (is not) a bag. | Is there a computer? | Yes, there is./No, there isn't. |
| **Plural** | There are some mats. | There aren't (are not) any mats. | Are there any posters? | Yes, there are./No, there aren't. |

| | | | | **Wh- questions** |
|---|---|---|---|---|
| | | | | How many students are there? |

## Vocabulary – Furniture

**1** Look at the photo opposite of Torin's classroom in Samoa and read what she says. Is it different to your classroom?

Hi! My name's Torin Lagavale.
I'm fourteen and I'm from Samoa.
There are 300 students in my school
and there are seventeen students in
my class. There's a photo of my
classroom on page twenty-five.
There aren't any desks or chairs – we
are on mats on the floor. The
teacher's table and chair are behind
the students. There are two big
windows and there's a big blackboard.
There aren't any computers. How many
students are there in your class?

Torin

**2** Are these things in Torin's classroom?

desks   mats   chairs   windows
blackboard   computers

**3** Match the words to the numbers in the photo on page 25. Which 5 things are not in the photo?

window *(1)* desk   floor   wall
shelf/shelves   table   cupboard   poster
wastebin   blackboard   drawers   mat

**4** Complete the sentences. Use *there's* or *there are*.

1 *There's* a teacher in the classroom.
2 … some mats on the floor.
3 … a student in front of the teacher.
4 … some posters on the wall.
5 … a table on the right.
6 … two big windows.

**5** Look at the photo and correct the sentences.

1 There are some drawers in Torin's classroom.

*There aren't any drawers in Torin's classroom.*

2 There are three students in the photo.
3 There are some shelves.
4 There are five desks.
5 There's a computer.
6 There's a wastebin.

**6** In pairs, ask and answer about the photo. Use these words.

students   teacher   shelves   doors
tables   computer   blackboard

A: Are there any students?
B: Yes, there are.
A: How many students are there?
B: Seventeen.

# FOCUS 5 Communication – Describe things and places

My classroom

## Vocabulary – Prepositions of place

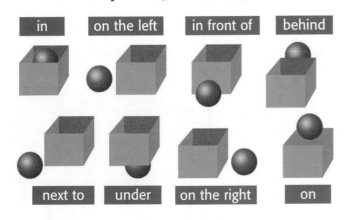

| in | on the left | in front of | behind |
| --- | --- | --- | --- |

| next to | under | on the right | on |
| --- | --- | --- | --- |

**1** Look at the photo of Torin's classroom again. Complete the sentences.

1  The posters are **on** the wall.
2  The teacher's table is … the students.
3  There are windows on the right and … of the classroom.
4  A student is … the blackboard.
5  The blackboard is … the teacher's desk.
6  The students are … the floor.

## Find out!

**2** Student A look at the photo on this page. Student B look at the photo on page 134. Find the differences.

**A:** Are there books in your picture?
**B:** Yes, there are./No, there aren't.
**A:** Where are they?
**B:** On the shelf.
**A:** How many students are there?
**B:** Nine.

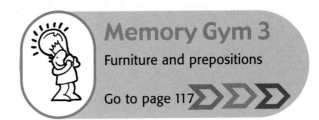

Memory Gym 3

Furniture and prepositions

Go to page 117

This is me

Entrance to South Pole Centre

This is my room. Cosy!

My room from the other end.

Room 14
Amundsen-Scott
South Pole Centre
South Pole
Antarctic

Dear Francesca,

Thank you for your e-mail. How are you? There are thirty people here at the South Pole in winter – I'm a scientist here. It's dark and it's very cold – minus fifty degrees Centigrade! The Antarctic isn't white – it's blue!

Here are three photos of my room. It's very small but it's my home!

My bed is on the left, and there's a desk with a chair under the bed. On the walls there are photos of my friends and family and lots of postcards. My favourite things are postcards from warm places – Rio de Janeiro, Sydney, Rome, San Francisco!

My books, cassettes and CDs are on the shelves. Some of the shelves are on the wall on the right, and some are under my bed.

Behind the door on the left there's a big cupboard. My bags are in it. Next to the bed there's a small white door and there's a table in front of it. In the morning the floor is very cold, but there's a mat to stand on. It's a present from my girlfriend in Germany.

Write to me again soon!

Best wishes,

Hi, it's me!

Robert

# FOCUS 6 Skills – A room in the Antarctic

## Study skills – Reading

**Prediction**

Predicting helps you read more easily.

- Before you read a text, look at the pictures, design and title.
- What's the topic of the text?
- What do you know about the topic?

## Reading

**1** Think about the study skill. Then look at the text quickly (but don't read it) and answer the questions.

1 What text type is it?
2 What's the topic?
3 Write three things you know about the Antarctic.

**2** Quick Read. Check your ideas from exercise 1.

**3** Find and check these words in the text.

| winter | small | bed | warm | present |

**4** Detailed Read. Read the text again and answer the questions.

1 Is Robert Schwarz a teacher? *No*
2 How many people are there at the South Pole?
3 Where is his desk?
4 Where are his books?
5 Are these things in the room? Yes ✓ or no ✗ ?

a door ✓          a wastebin
shelves           a chair
a window          a desk
drawers           a bed
a table           a cupboard

## Listening

**5** Isabel is moving into a new room. Copy the plan of her room. Then listen and draw the furniture in the correct places.

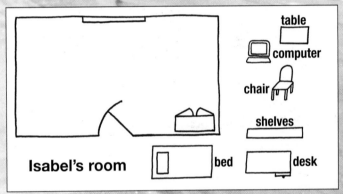

## Speaking

**6** Draw 2 plans of your room.
Draw plan 1 with the furniture (this is secret).
Draw plan 2 with windows and doors only.

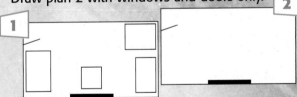

**7** In pairs, give plan 2 to your partner. Student A describe your room. Student B draw the furniture in the room.

A: My bed's behind the door.
B: Is it on the left, next to the window?
A: Yes, it is.

## Writing Gym 2

A letter about your room

Go to page 125 ⟫⟫⟫

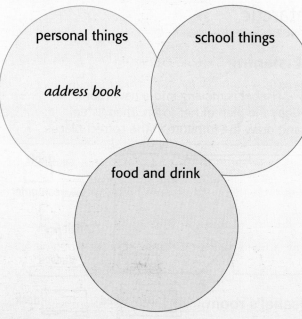

# Energy Check

## Vocabulary

**1** Put the words into the correct groups.

> address book   camera   ruler
> ID card   key   mobile   notebook
> orange   pen   pencil   passport
> crisps   wallet   bottle of cola

**personal things**

*address book*

**school things**

**food and drink**

**2** Make the words plural.

1 a guitar *guitars*
2 a camera
3 a key
4 a man
5 a child
6 this

7 an orange
8 an apple
9 an envelope
10 a woman
11 a person
12 that

**3** Where's Spot? Find the answers.

1 *Spot's in the box.*

## Grammar

**4** Put the possessive 's into the correct places.

1 Toms bag   *Tom's bag.*
2 my mothers camera
3 Isabels parents
4 Mels friend
5 Richards photo
6 Francescas friends

**5** Choose the correct words.

1 This is/These are a photo of my classroom.
2 There is/There are sixteen students in my class.
3 There are/There is a window in the room.
4 There isn't/There aren't any computers.
5 Those are/That is my book.
6 Are there/Is there any computers in your class?
7 How many students is there/are there?
8 Is there/Are there a CD player in your room?

## Communication

**6** Match the questions to the correct answers.

| 1 Is there a computer in your class? | a) thirty-five |
| 2 Where is it? | b) Yes, there is. |
| 3 How many students are there in your class? | c) Mrs Sanuri |
| 4 What's your teacher's name? | d) on the teacher's table |

| How RU doing? | | 😁 | 😐 | 😟 |
|---|---|---|---|---|
| | Vocabulary Exercises 1–3 | | | |
| | Grammar Exercises 4,5 | | | |
| | Communication Exercise 6 | | | |

# Blue

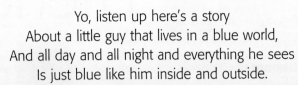

## da ba dee ...

Yo, listen up here's a story
About a little guy that lives in a blue world,
And all day and all night and everything he sees
Is just blue like him inside and outside.

Blue his 1 _house_ with a blue little 2 …
And a blue Corvette,
And everything is blue for him and himself
And everybody around
'Cause he ain't got nobody to listen to.

I'm blue a ba dee da ba dai
Da ba dee da ba dai
Da ba dee da ba dai
Da ba dee da ba dai
Da ba dee da ba dai
Da ba dee da ba dai
Da ba dee da ba dai

I have a blue 3 … with a blue window,
Blue is the 4 … of all that I wear.
Blue are the 5 … and all the trees are too,
I have a 6 … and she is so blue.

Blue are the 7 … here that walk around,
Blue like my Corvette, it's in and outside.
Blue are the 8 … I say and what I think,
Blue are the feelings that live inside me.

I'm blue, a ba dee da ba dai

ain't got = hasn't got

Eiffel 65 is the name of a band from Turin in Italy. There are three people in the band – Maurizio Lobina, Jeffrey Jey and DJ Gabry Ponte. They are the writers of the hit *Blue* – Number 1 in Britain, France, Canada, Spain, Australia and many other countries.

' Blue is a universal colour for us. It's the colour of the sea, the sky, the Earth. It's also the colour of a feeling. ' Eiffel 65.

**1** Listen. Do you know this song?

**2** Put the words in the correct places.

| house x2   people   streets |
| colour   window   words   girlfriend |

**3** Now listen and check.

**4** What do you think? In this song, is blue a happy colour or a sad colour? Why is the man in the song blue?

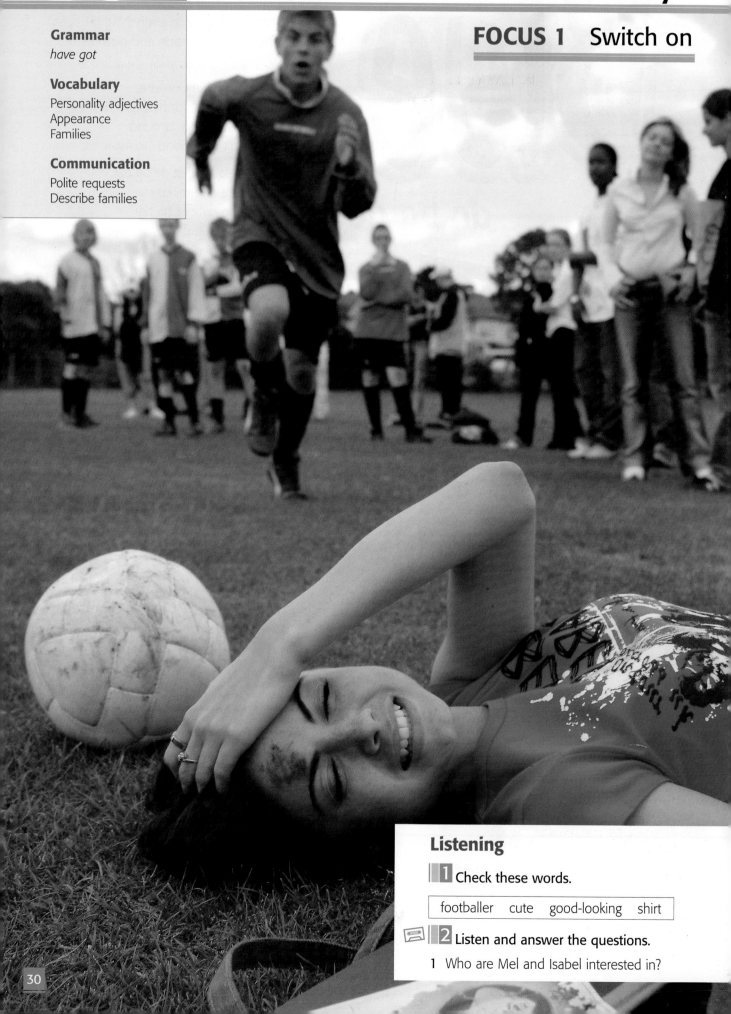

# Friends and family

**Grammar**
*have got*

**Vocabulary**
Personality adjectives
Appearance
Families

**Communication**
Polite requests
Describe families

## FOCUS 1  Switch on

### Listening

**1** Check these words.

footballer  cute  good-looking  shirt

**2** Listen and answer the questions.

1  Who are Mel and Isabel interested in?

## Reading

| | |
|---|---|
| **Isabel** | How many brothers and sisters have you got, Mel? |
| **Mel** | I've got a brother called Luke and a sister called Ann. Hey, look! There's Mickey Kelly! |
| **Isabel** | Who's Mickey Kelly? |
| **Mel** | He's a really good footballer and … he's cute. |
| **Isabel** | Cute? Where is he? What does he look like? |
| **Mel** | He's good-looking – he's got blond hair and green eyes. He's number ten. |
| **Isabel** | Oh, yes! Has he got a girlfriend? |
| **Mel** | No, he hasn't. |
| **Isabel** | Who's that? |
| **Mel** | The girl with long brown hair and the pink shirt? |
| **Isabel** | Yes, the film star. |
| **Mel** | Ooh, Isabel! That's his sister, Maria. She's really friendly. Look out! |

# OUCH!!

| | |
|---|---|
| **Mickey** | I'm really sorry! Can I help? |
| **Mel** | Yes. Can you pick 'up her books, please? |
| **Mickey** | Yes, sure. Are you OK? |
| **Isabel** | Yes, thanks. Hey, Mel, he's the cute footballer! |
| **Mel** | Come on, Isabel, let's go! |

### 3 Read and choose the correct words.

1 Mel's brother is called Mickey/Luke/Ann.
2 Mel's sister is called Isabel/Ann/Maria.
3 Mickey's hair is red/black/blond.
4 Mickey's eyes are black/blue/green.
5 Mickey's sister is called Mel/Ann/Maria.

## Roleplay – Polite requests

### 4 Put the sentences into the correct order.

1 A: you/please/me/can/help/?

*Can you help me, please?*

  B: I/can't/sorry/I'm/.

2 A: name/please/spell/you/can/your/?
  B: sure/yes/.

### 5 Student A ask student B for help to do these things.

- say that again
- open the window
- spell your name
- close the door
- help me
- pick up those bags

**A:** Can you say that again, please?
**B:** Yes, sure.

## Vocabulary – Personality adjectives

### 6 Choose the correct adjective for each picture.

*friendly/unfriendly*

*confident/shy*

*noisy/quiet*

*happy/sad*

### 7 In pairs, describe yourself and a friend.

*I'm a bit shy, but I think I'm friendly and … .*
*Margaret's very noisy and she's … .*

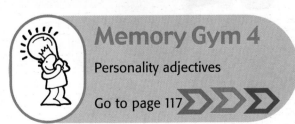

**Memory Gym 4**

Personality adjectives

Go to page 117

# FOCUS 2  Vocabulary – Appearance

1 Work out the meaning of the words.

2 Use the words to describe the photos.

good looking

MOUSTACHE

bald

BLONDE HAIR

BEARD

TALL

DARK HAIR

BROWN EYES

FAT

young

SLIM

LONG HAIR

GREY HAIR

Yoda

Will Smith

Lisa Kudrow

Pavarotti

Olive Oyl

Mini-Me and Dr Evil

GREEN EYES

glasses

STRAIGHT HAIR

SHORT HAIR

Beautiful

old

RED HAIR

# FOCUS 3  Grammar – *have got*

| Positive | Negative | Questions | Short answers |
|---|---|---|---|
| I've/you've got<br>he's/she's/it's got<br>we've/they've got | I/you haven't got<br>he/she/it hasn't got<br>we/they haven't got | Have I/you got ...?<br>Has he/she/it got ...?<br>Have we/they got ...? | Yes, I have./No, I haven't.<br>Yes, you have./No, you haven't.<br>Yes, he has./No, he hasn't. |
| *He's got blue eyes.* | *She hasn't got blond hair.* | *Has he got a beard?* | **Wh-** questions |
|  |  |  | *What colour eyes has he got?*<br>*What sort of hair has she got?* |

**1** Match the descriptions to the photos on page 32.

a) She's tall and slim. She's got black hair and brown eyes.
b) They're short and fat. They're bald, and they haven't got beards or moustaches.
c) He isn't slim. He's got black hair and brown eyes. He's old.

**2** Make questions about the people in the photos on page 32. Then add 4 more questions and answer them.

1  Will Smith/beard?

*Has Will Smith got a beard?*
*No, he hasn't.*

2  Olive Oyl/red hair?
3  Dr Evil/a beard?
4  Will Smith/glasses?

**3** Correct the sentences. Write true sentences.

1  Pavarotti's got blond hair.

*No, he hasn't. He's got black hair.*

2  Will Smith's got blond hair.
3  Lisa Kudrow's got curly hair.
4  Yoda's got blue eyes.
5  Dr Evil's got hair.

**4** In pairs, look at the photos. Student A make a false sentence. Student B correct the information.

A: Lisa Kudrow's got black hair.
B: No, she hasn't. She's got blond hair.

**Think about language**

**Make rules.**

- *She's tall.*
  *'s* means is/has

- *She's got blond hair.*
  *'s* means is/has

**5** Read exercise 1 again and answer the questions.

1  Which *'s* means *has*?
2  Which *'s* means *is*?

**6** Put the words into the correct groups.

| brown eyes | tall | slim | short |
|---|---|---|---|
| brown hair | fat | glasses | |

| has got | is |
|---|---|
| *brown eyes* | *tall* |

## Speaking

**7** Student A think of someone famous. Student B ask questions. Who is it?

A: Is it a girl?
B: Yes, it is.
A: Has she got brown hair?
B: Yes, she has.
A: What sort of hair has she got?

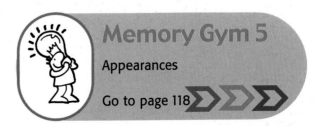

Memory Gym 5

Appearances

Go to page 118

I've got a big family. I've got fifteen or sixteen cousins in the USA! This is a photo of my family on my birthday. My grandmother's called Anna and my grandfather's called Bill. They're Irish. My mum is their daughter. She's called Patricia. My dad's called Joe.

I've got a brother called Liam (he's only eight years old) and two sisters called Maria and Teresa. Maria's got long, brown hair and she's really confident. Teresa has got blond hair and she's quiet.

Teresa's husband is called Paul. They've got a new baby called Emma. She's beautiful. I'm her uncle.

NOTE BOOK

baby Emma

**1** Read about Mickey's family. Then find the correct words to complete the list.

| mother | father |
|---|---|
| *mum* | dad |
| grandmother | |
| wife | |
| | brother |
| | son |
| aunt | |
| cousin | cousin |
| girlfriend | boyfriend |
| He's engaged/married/divorced. | |

**2** Read Mickey's description again. One person from the letter isn't in the photo. What is his/her name?

**3** Answer the questions about Mickey's family.

1 Who is Patricia's husband?
2 Who is Liam's grandfather?
3 Who are Emma's parents?
4 Who is Emma's aunt?
5 Who is Emma's grandmother?

## Memory Tip 3

**Use English to describe you.**

• Think about your life in English.

*I've got two brothers. My father's name is ...*

## Pronunciation – /θ/, /ð/

 **4** Listen and repeat.

/ð/ mo**th**er **th**is
/θ/ **th**ree **th**irty

 **5** Listen and put the words into the correct columns.

| thirteen these thin brother three those father that they birthday | |
|---|---|
| /θ/ | /ð/ |
| thirteen | these |

## Memory Gym 6

Families

Go to page 118 ▷▷▷

---

# FOCUS 5   Communication – Families

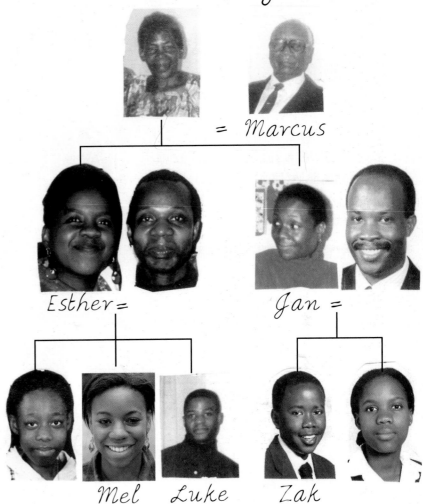

Mel's Family Tree

= Marcus

Esther =          Jan =

Mel    Luke    Zak

## Find out!

**1** Student A look at this family tree. Student B look at page 134. Ask questions to complete Mel's family tree.

A: What's Mel's father called?
B: Louis. What's her mother called?

## Listening

**2** Listen to Mel and check the family tree.

## Speaking

**3** In pairs, ask your partner about his/her family or a friend's family. Draw a family tree.

• What's your mum's/dad's name?
• Have you got any brothers/sisters?
• What does he/she look like?
• What are they called?

*Remember*

*he's got = he has got*

*he's = he is*

# STAR WARS

## NAME LUKE SKYWALKER

He's tall and he's got blond hair and blue eyes. He's 1.72 metres tall. He's intelligent and quiet, but not very confident. His best friend is his teacher, Yoda. There are three other people in his family – his sister, his father and mother.

## NAME

| | |
|---|---|
| Appearance | tall, slim, gold |
| Height | 1.67 metres |
| Other | good at languages, noisy, not confident, says 'oh dear' when worried |

## NAME

| | |
|---|---|
| Appearance | small, fat, white and blue |
| Height | 0.96 metres |
| Other | cute, intelligent and quiet |

## NAME

| | |
|---|---|
| Appearance | very tall, has got a black mask |
| Height | 1.85 metres |
| Favourite colour | black |
| Other | very confident and unfriendly, hasn't got many friends |

## NAME

| | |
|---|---|
| Appearance | tall, slim, long dark hair, brown eyes |
| Height | 1.5 metres |
| Other | Luke's twin sister, very confident and intelligent, but quiet |

**Darth Vader**

C3PO

R2D2

**STRANGE BUT TRUE**
The director of *Star Wars* is George Lucas. His office is at Skywalker Ranch in California.

**Princess Leia**

**Luke Skywalker**

# FOCUS 6   Skills – The *Star Wars* family

## Reading

**1** Quick Read. Read the descriptions and match them to the correct *Star Wars* characters.

**2** Detailed Read. Read the descriptions again and answer the questions.

1  Who has got blond hair?   *Luke Skywalker*
2  Who has got blue eyes?
3  Who is Luke's sister?
4  Who is tall, slim and gold?
5  What colour is Darth Vader's mask?
6  Who hasn't got many friends?
7  What colour is R2D2?
8  What is George Lucas's office called?

## Listening

**3** Listen and match the descriptions to the correct pictures.

## Speaking

**4** Think of 1 or 2 friends in your class. Complete the table about them.

| Age | 13 |
| --- | --- |
| Appearance | *tall, slim, grey eyes* |
| Favourite things | |
| Other | |

**5** In groups, ask and answer. Find the person. (Don't say the person's name!)

- How old is … ?
- Has he/she got … ?
- What is his/her favourite … ?
- What colour … ?
- Is your person … ?

### Study skills – Writing

**Write a draft**
Make notes to work out your ideas first.
- Write a draft.
- Check the spelling, vocabulary and grammar.
- Then write it in your notebook.

**6** Check the text and correct the mistakes. The mistakes are <u>underlined</u>.

<u>He twelve</u> ➔ *He's twelve*

#### Tommy

<u>He twelve</u>, he's tall and <u>he got</u> black hair. <u>He</u> nickname is 'Tombo'. He <u>have</u> intelligent, but he isn't good at school. His favourite TV programme <u>are</u> *Friends*. <u>There is</u> four people in his family.

## Writing Gym 3

A description of a person

Go to page 126 ▷▷▷

37

# Energy Check

## Grammar

**1** Choose the correct words.

1 They has got/have got a little sister.
2 Liam hasn't got/haven't got long hair.
3 Have/Has Tom got a sister?
4 My dad has got/have got a moustache.
5 Mel hasn't got/haven't got blue eyes.
6 I has got/have got a sister called Madelaine.
7 What colour eyes have/has you got?
8 What sort of hair have/has she got?

**2** Make questions with *have got*.

1 what sort of hair/your teacher?

*What sort of hair has your teacher got?*

2 Mel/any brothers or sisters?
3 you/a mobile?
4 what colour eyes/you?
5 your best friend/blond hair?
6 we/English homework today?

**3** Write true answers for the questions in exercise 2.

*1 He/She's got black hair.*

## Vocabulary

**4** Complete the sentences.

1 My father's brother is my  *uncle* .
2 My mother's daughter is my … .
3 My father's son is my … .
4 My mother's sister is my … .
5 My father's mother is my … .
6 My mother's father is my … .
7 My uncle's son is my … .
8 My aunt's daughter is my … .

**5** Complete the conversation about Marco with the correct adjectives. You don't agree with your friend Lisa.

Lisa    Marco's friendly.
You     He isn't! He's ¹ *unfriendly* !
Lisa    He's shy.
You     He isn't! He's ²… !
Lisa    And he's quiet.
You     He isn't quiet! He's ³… !
Lisa    Marco's a happy person.
You     I think he's ⁴… !

**6** Complete the sentences with *is* or *has got*.

1 He *has got* a beard.
2 He … a moustache.
3 He … bald.
4 He … curly hair.
5 He … fat.
6 He … good-looking.
7 She … glasses.
8 She … long, blond hair.
9 She … short.
10 She … short, grey hair.
11 She … slim.
12 She … tall.

**7** Describe the people. Use the correct words from exercise 6.

*1 He's got … and he's … .*

## Communication

**8** Put the sentences into the correct order.

1 A: please/help/you/can/me/?

*Can you help me, please?*

   B: sure/yes/.

2 A: can/open/this/door/you/please/?
   B: can't/sorry/I'm/I/.

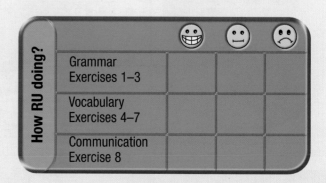

| How RU doing? | | 😁 | 😐 | 😞 |
|---|---|---|---|---|
| | Grammar Exercises 1–3 | | | |
| | Vocabulary Exercises 4–7 | | | |
| | Communication Exercise 8 | | | |

cool = great

Brownie

**3** I love music too and my favourite CD is by Destiny's Child. It's called Independent Women. It's old but it's cool. I've got a lot of CDs – about 150!

DESTINY'S CHILD

INDEPENDENT WOMEN PART I

**2** My cool new mobile phone is one of my favourite things too. It's a birthday present from my grandmother. I'm on the phone a lot!

**4** Have I got a computer? No, I haven't, but my brother has. He's got the Internet too but computers are boring!

**1** I'm Lucy, I'm fifteen and I'm from Glasgow in Scotland. What are my favourite things? Well, first is my dog, Brownie. She's a sausage dog and she's really cute. I love animals.

## Culture FiLe

**In Britain**

- ✪ Five million people have got a dog.
- ✪ 66% teenagers have got a mobile phone.
- ✪ 47% of teenagers have got a computer.
- ✪ 61% of teenagers are on the Internet.

## QueStioNS

**1** Read about Lucy and answer *true* (T) or *false* (F).

1 Lucy has got a dog.
2 Her phone is a present from her brother.
3 Lucy's favourite CD is new.
4 66% of British teenagers have got a mobile phone.

**2** In groups, discuss the questions.

1 What are your favourite things, and why? (Compare your list with other students.)
2 How many people in your class have got a dog?
3 How many of your friends have got a mobile phone or a computer?

RETRO 72 TEAM

# Projects

## My Cartoon Character

**Project 1**  Create a Cartoon Character or a TV Character.

**1** Complete a factfile for your character. Then use your factfile to write about your character. You can create a normal or crazy character.

| Character factfile | |
|---|---|
| Cartoon character or TV personality | |
| Animal or a human? | |
| Name | |
| Nickname | |
| Background *Where is he/she from? (planet, country, town?)* | |
| Age | |
| Appearance *What does he/she/it look like? Is his/her appearance strange? (hair, eyes, body)* | |
| Personality *(happy, shy, unfriendly?)* | |
| Family and friends *Describe your character's family and friends.* | |
| Favourite expression | |
| Favourite things | |

**2** Draw your cartoon character (or ask a cool friend to draw it). Or make your TV character from magazines.

# Project 2
## Create a storyboard.

1. Think of a short scene for your character to appear in. First draw some simple pictures to show the events in your scene.

2. Create the storyboard for your scene. What do the characters say? Write the conversation under each picture.

3. Practise your scene. Then act it out for the class.

1. The phone! The phone!

2. Where is it? Where is it?

3. CRASH!!

4. Hi! we're not at home... BEEP! Hello. This is Anna. Please call me.

UNIT 4

# Daily life

**Grammar**
Present simple

**Vocabulary**
Time
Daily activity verbs

**Communication**
Talk about times
Talk about daily routines
Phone the cinema

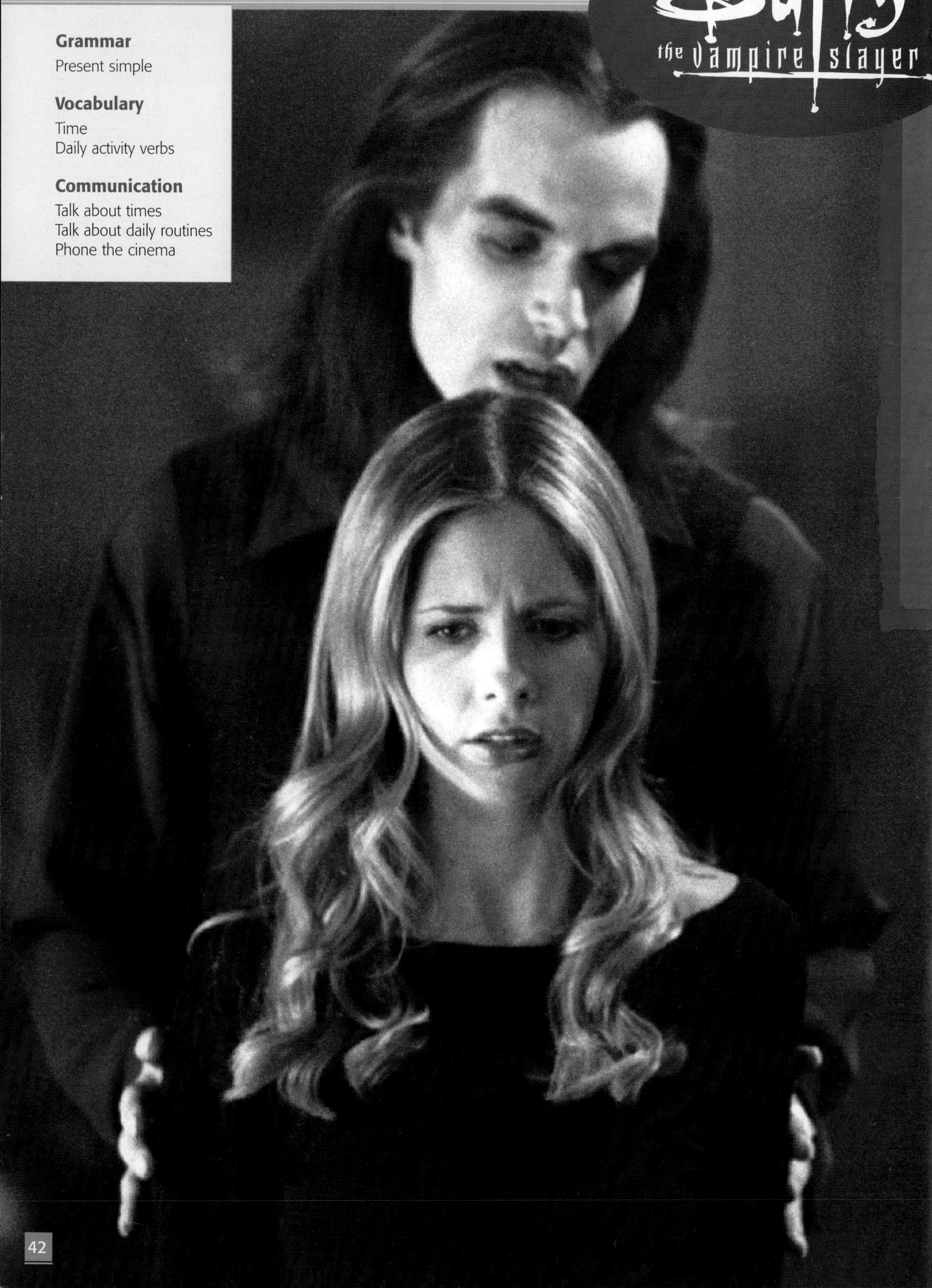
Buffy
the vampire slayer

It's eleven o'clock at night in Sunnydale, California, and Buffy Summers starts work. She studies at college in the morning but she doesn't like college work. At night she kills vampires. Why does she kill vampires? Because she's the main character in the TV programme, Buffy the Vampire Slayer.

In real life, Buffy is the actress Sarah Michelle Gellar from New York. Sarah has got green eyes and blond hair. Her favourite food is pasta and her favourite colour is red.

Sarah works a lot. She starts work at six o'clock in the morning and finishes at nine o'clock in the evening. She's an athlete too. She goes to the gym and she plays football. She doesn't smoke.

Does she live with her family? No, she doesn't. She lives in Los Angeles with her dog, Thor.

# FOCUS 1   Switch on

## Reading

**1** Check these words.

| start | work | study | like | kill |
|-------|------|-------|------|------|
| finish | go | smoke | live | |

**2** Read and answer the questions.

1  Who is Buffy Summers?
2  Who is Sarah Michelle Gellar?
3  Where's Sarah from?
4  What colour is her hair?
5  What's her favourite food?
6  What's her favourite colour?
7  Where is her home now?
8  What's her dog's name?

**3** Put the phrases into the correct order of time.

| at night | in the evening |
|----------|----------------|
| in the afternoon | in the morning |

*1  in the morning*

## Vocabulary – Time

**What time is it?**

It's three **o'clock**.          It's half **past** three.
It's five **past** three.         It's twenty-five **to** four.
It's ten **past** three.          It's twenty **to** four.
It's twenty-five **past** three.  It's quarter **to** four.
It's twenty **past** three.       It's ten **to** four.
It's quarter **past** three.      It's five **to** four.

**4** Find these times in the text.

**5** In pairs, ask and tell the time.

A: Excuse me. What time is it?
B: It's ten o'clock./I'm sorry, I don't know.
A: Thank you.

| 1 | 10.00 | 4 | 2.35 | 7 | 6.20 |
|---|-------|---|------|---|------|
| 2 | 11.15 | 5 | 3.25 | 8 | 9.05 |
| 3 | 11.45 | 6 | 8.50 | 9 | the correct time now |

**6** In pairs, ask and answer about the times of the planes from Sunnydale Airport.

A: What time is the plane to …?
B: It's at … .

### Flights from Sunnydale Airport

| New York | 7.00 |
|----------|------|
| Los Angeles | 8.10 |
| Detroit | 9.40 |
| San Francisco | 11.30 |
| Washington | 12.55 |
| Chicago | 1.50 |

# FOCUS 2  Grammar – Present simple *he/she/it*

| Positive | Negative | Questions | Short answers |
|---|---|---|---|
| He<br>She } works.<br>It | He<br>She } doesn't work.<br>It | Does { he<br>she<br>it } work? | Yes, he does./No, he doesn't. |
| *Sarah works a lot.* | *She doesn't smoke.* | *Does she live with her family?* | **Wh- questions**<br>*Why does she kill vampires?* |

### Think about language

**Look at the examples.**

**Positive** *She lives with her parents.*

| Negative | Questions |
|---|---|
| *She doesn't live with her parents.* | *Does she live with her parents?* |

**1** Look at the text about Buffy on page 43. Find the present simple verbs (not *'s* or *'s got*).

### Memory Tip 4

**Make strange connections.**

*sssss*

Present simple he/she/it =

She work**s** in Sunnydale.

**2** Complete with the correct form of the verbs.

**Series of the week**

*Angel, Saturday 11pm, BBC2*

**NEW!**
★★★★★

In series one of *Buffy the Vampire Slayer*, Buffy
¹ (work) _works_ with a character called Angel.
Angel ² (live) … in Sunnydale, but he
³ (not go) … to college and he ⁴ (not work) … .
He's a vampire – the only good vampire in the
world. He ⁵ (like) … Buffy and she
⁶ (like) … Angel. He ⁷ (not go) … out in the
morning or afternoon because he ⁸ (not like) …
the light – it ⁹ (kill) … vampires. He only
¹⁰ (go) … out at night.

**3** Correct the sentences. Write true sentences.

1 Buffy Summers lives in Los Angeles.

*She doesn't live in Los Angeles. She lives in Sunnydale.*

2 She studies in the evening.
3 She likes college work.
4 Sarah Michelle Gellar lives in New York.
5 Sarah starts work at eleven o'clock.
6 She lives with her family.
7 Angel lives in Los Angeles.
8 He goes out in the morning.

**4** Match the questions to the correct answers.

| | |
|---|---|
| 1 Where does Angel live? | a) at night |
| 2 Does he go to work? | b) Sunnydale |
| 3 Does he like Buffy? | c) Yes, he does. |
| 4 When does he go out? | d) because the light kills vampires |
| 5 Why does he only go out at night? | e) No, he doesn't. |

**5** In pairs, ask and answer about Buffy and Sarah Michelle Gellar.

1 where/Buffy/live?

A: Where does Buffy live?
B: She lives in California.

2 where/Sarah Michelle Gellar/live?
3 where/Buffy/go/in the morning?
4 what/Buffy/do/at night?
5 Sarah/live with her family?
6 Sarah/like dogs?

# A Day in the Life of Mel Williams

**1** Look at the pictures of Mel's day. Match the words to the correct pictures.

| | |
|---|---|
| go to bed | have breakfast |
| finish school | get up ① |
| do homework | start school |
| watch TV | have dinner |

**2** In groups, check your answers.

*1 She gets up.*

## Pronunciation – /s/, /z/, /ɪz/

**3** Listen and repeat the verbs.

starts plays watches kills works finishes
smokes gets up goes does runs studies

**4** Now listen again and put the verbs into the correct columns.

| /s/ | /z/ | /ɪz/ |
|---|---|---|
| *starts* | *plays* | *watches* |

## Listening

**5** In pairs, guess the times for Mel's daily activities.

A: I think she gets up at quarter to seven.
B: I think she … at … .

**6** Listen to a description of Mel's day. Check your guesses from exercise 5.

**7** In pairs, ask and answer questions about Mel's day.

A: What time does Mel get up?
B: She gets up at quarter to seven.
A: What time does Mel … ?

**Memory Gym 7**

Daily activity verbs

Go to page 119

45

# FOCUS 4   Grammar – Present simple *I/you/we/they*

| Positive | Negative | Questions | Short answers |
|---|---|---|---|
| I/You We/They } work. | I/You We/They } don't work. | Do { I/you we/they } work? | Yes, I do./No, I don't. |
| I work at night. | I don't work at night. | Do they work at night? | **Wh- questions** |
| | | | Where do you work? What time do they get up? |

**Think about language**

**Make a rule.**

The **I, you, we** and **they** forms of the Present simple are the same/different.

**1** Check these verbs. Then complete the text with the correct forms.

| start | go | get up | give | get |
|---|---|---|---|---|
| walk | deliver | do | have | finish |

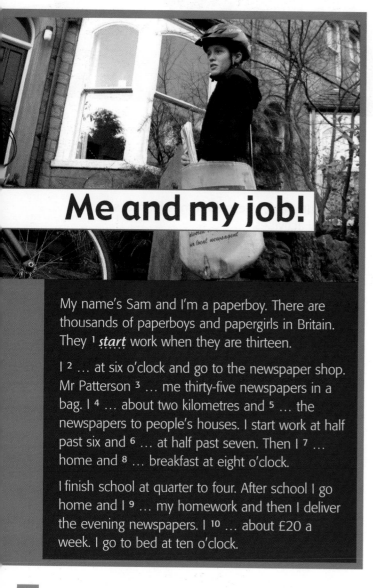

# Me and my job!

My name's Sam and I'm a paperboy. There are thousands of paperboys and papergirls in Britain. They ¹ *start* work when they are thirteen.

I ² … at six o'clock and go to the newspaper shop. Mr Patterson ³ … me thirty-five newspapers in a bag. I ⁴ … about two kilometres and ⁵ … the newspapers to people's houses. I start work at half past six and ⁶ … at half past seven. Then I ⁷ … home and ⁸ … breakfast at eight o'clock.

I finish school at quarter to four. After school I go home and I ⁹ … my homework and then I deliver the evening newspapers. I ¹⁰ … about £20 a week. I go to bed at ten o'clock.

**2** Listen and check your answers to exercise 1.

**3** Make questions for Sam's answers.

1   I get up at six o'clock.

*What time do you get up?*

2   I start work at half past six.
3   at half past seven
4   I have breakfast at eight o'clock.
5   at quarter to four
6   at ten o'clock

**4** In pairs, take turns to ask Sam questions and answer.

1   get up/at nine o'clock?

A: Sam, do you get up at nine o'clock?
B: No, I don't. I get up at six.

2   finish work/at seven o'clock?
3   have breakfast/in the shop?
4   finish school/at four o'clock?
5   do homework/at school?
6   go to bed/at nine o'clock

**5** Choose the correct words.

1   I work/works in a shop.
2   They don't/doesn't go to this school.
3   We likes/like that book.
4   Do you lives/live here?
5   What time do you gets/get up?
6   We don't/doesn't go to school.
7   Where do/does they live?
8   They has/have breakfast at half past eight.

Remember

go to work
go to school
go to bed
go home

# FOCUS 5 Communication – Daily routine, Phone the cinema

**1** Complete the chart with the correct times for your daily routine.

| | My day | My partner's day |
|---|---|---|
| get up | | |
| have breakfast | | |
| go to school | | |
| start school | | |
| finish school | | |
| go home | | |
| do homework | | |
| watch TV | | |
| go to bed | | |
| Any other activities? | | |

**2** In pairs, interview your partner and complete the chart.

A: What time do you get up?
B: I get up at ... .

**3** In groups, talk about the differences between you and your partner.

*I get up at seven o'clock but Michel gets up at eight.*

**Roleplay – Phone the cinema**

**4** Listen and complete. Then in pairs, practise the conversation.

Jack      ¹ *Hello* . Is that the cinema?
Cinema   Yes, it is.
Jack      What ² ... does *Spiderman* start?
Cinema   It starts at ³...... .
Jack      What time does it ⁴... ?
Cinema   It finishes at ⁵...... .
Jack      Thank you very much.
Cinema   You're ⁶... .

**5** In pairs, phone the cinema and ask for information about *Terminator* and *Lord of the Rings III*.

**Find out!**

**6** Student A look at this page. Student B look at page 135. Complete the missing information.

A: What time does *The Simpsons* start?
B: It starts at ... .

| **Friday**    19th July |
|---|
| **BBC1** |
| **6.00**    **Friends** The one where Ross meets a new girlfriend. |
| **...**      **The Simpsons** |
| **6.50**    **Top of the Pops** With Oasis and Dido. |
| **...**      **Football Focus** |
| **8.30**    **Film: The Beach** Starring Leonardo DiCaprio |
| **...**      **Night Music** |

Eduardo cooks the sap. It's called chicle.

## Eduardo the Chiclero

Eduardo and his family are from Guatemala in Central America. Eduardo is a chiclero – he makes chewing gum. Eduardo makes the gum from Sapodilla trees in the rainforest.

He climbs a tree and cuts it. The sap from the tree goes into Eduardo's bag. The sap is called chicle. Chicle is the original chewing gum.

Eduardo climbs trees all day, so he knows every tree in the rainforest! It is hard work. He gets up at half past five in the morning and has breakfast. He starts work at six o'clock and he finishes at five o'clock in the evening.

After five days in the forest, Eduardo and the other chicleros go home with their bags of chicle. They cook the sap and make the chicle gum.

www.junglegum.com

The gum in this 'Chewing Gum Kit' is chicle gum from the rainforest in Guatemala. Chicle gum helps the rainforest because it gives work to Eduardo and the chicleros.

## Reading

**1** Check these words.

| tree | rainforest | climb |
| cut | sap | original | cook |

**2** Quick Read. Read about Eduardo and answer true or false.

1 Eduardo lives in Central America. ✔
2 He's a student.
3 He works in a factory.
4 Chicle comes from trees.
5 Chicle makes chewing gum.

**3** Detailed Read. Read the text again and answer the questions.

1 Where does Eduardo work?
2 What time does he start work?
3 What time does he finish work?
4 How do the chicleros make the chicle gum?
5 What sort of gum is in the 'Chewing Gum Kit'?
6 Is American gum from trees or factories?

He climbs the Sapodilla tree

In one year, people in the USA eat 10 millon kilometres of chewing gum, but they eat gum from factories. It isn't chicle gum from trees.

## Study skills – Listening

**Get ready to listen**

Before you listen, focus on what you want to know.
- Look at the questions before you listen.
- Don't try to understand everything.

## Listening

**4** Check these words.

| taxi driver | doctor | farmer | am | pm |

**5** Listen. What are their names?

1

2

3

**6** Listen again and complete the table.

| Name | Suzanne | Nimmi | Richard |
|------|---------|-------|---------|
| get up | 1 **6pm** | 5 | 5am |
| have breakfast | 2 | 6 | 9 |
| start work | 8pm | 4.30am | 10 |
| finish work | 3 | 7 | 9pm |
| have dinner | 8.30am | 5pm | 11 |
| go to bed | 4 | 8 | 10pm |

## Speaking

**7** Student A choose one of the people from exercise 5. Student B interview your partner about his or her daily routine.

A: What time do you get up?
B: I get up at … .

### Writing Gym 4

A description of a daily routine.

Go to page 127 ▷▷▷ ▷▷▷

49

# Energy Check

## Grammar

**1** Complete with the correct form of the verbs.

1 You (arrive) _arrive_ at school at eight o'clock.
2 I (not go) … to bed at ten o'clock.
3 Tom and his dad (live) … in Manchester.
4 Tom (not go) … home after school.
5 We (start) … work at ten to nine.
6 Tom's dad (not work) … in the morning.
7 I (work) … at the university.
8 The film (finish) … at half past eight.
9 Sarah Gellar (not live) … with her family.

**2** Complete the questions with *do* or *does*.

1 _Does_ Tom play the piano?
2 What time … you have breakfast?
3 … Isabel's family live in Britain?
4 Where … her parents work?
5 … Angel like Buffy?
6 What time … we start work today?

**3** Make questions.

1 Isabel's family/live in Argentina?

*Do Isabel's family live in Argentina?*

2 where/you/live?
3 what time/your school/start?
4 Eduardo/work/in the rainforest?
5 what sport/Mickey/do?
6 what sport/you/do?
7 Buffy/hate vampires?
8 when/Angel/go out?

**4** Answer the questions in exercise 3.

*1 No, they don't.*

## Vocabulary

**5** Write the correct times.

*1 one o'clock*

**6** Put the daily activities into the correct order for a normal school day.

a) go home
b) do my homework
c) go to bed
d) get up ①
e) start school
f) finish school
g) watch TV
h) have breakfast
i) have dinner

**7** Write about your normal school day. Use the verbs in exercise 6.

*I get up at … and I have breakfast.*

## Communication

**8** Complete the conversation.

Julia   Hello. Is ¹ _that_ the ABC Cinema?
Cinema  Yes, ² … .
Julia   What time ³ … the film ⁴ … ?
Cinema  *Fluffy Heroes* or *Tubeway Terror*?
Julia   *Tubeway Terror*.
Cinema  It ⁵ … at half past eight.
Julia   And ⁶ …… does it ⁷ … ?
Cinema  ⁸ …… half past ten.
Julia   Thank you ⁹ …… .
Cinema  You're ¹⁰ … .

**9** Write the conversations.

1 A: Ask politely for the time.
  B: Give the correct time.
  A: Say 'thank you'.

  A: Excuse me …

2 A: Ask politely for the time.
  B: Apologise. You don't know.
  A: Say 'OK' and 'thank you'.

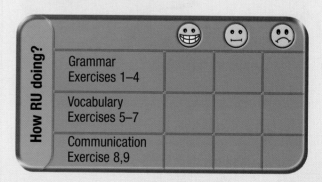

# Yellow Submarine

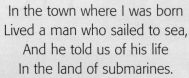

In the town where I was born
Lived a man who sailed to sea,
And he told us of his life
In the land of submarines.

So we sailed up to the sun
Till we found the sea of green,
And we lived beneath the waves
In our yellow submarine.

*We all live in our yellow submarine*
*Yellow submarine*
*Yellow submarine.*
*We all live in our yellow submarine*
*Yellow submarine*
*Yellow submarine.*

And our friends are all on board,
Many more of them live next door.
And the band begins to play.

*We all live in our yellow submarine*
*Yellow submarine …*

As we live a life of ease
Every one of us has all we need,
Sky of blue and sea of green
In our yellow submarine.

*We all live in our yellow submarine*
*Yellow submarine …*

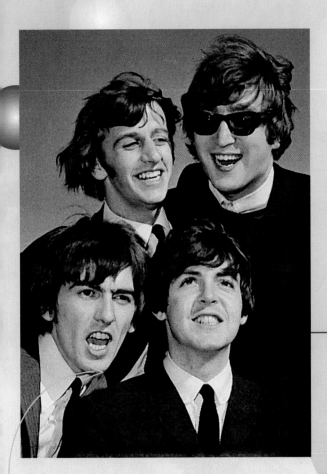

| The Beatles (1963 –1969) | John Lennon, Paul McCartney George Harrison Ringo Starr. |
|---|---|
| **Number one hits** | 17 in Britain, 20 in the USA |
| **First number one hit** | 1963 |
| **Last number one hit** | 1969 |
| **Yellow Submarine** | a number one hit in 1966. – a cartoon film in 1968. |

Other information: 'Ringo' means 'apple' in Japanese.
The Beatles' production company is called 'Apple'.

**1** Listen to the song. Do you know it?

**2** What do you know about the Beatles?

**3** Tick ✔ the sounds you hear.

a guitar   drums   a bell   a foghorn

a piano   the sea   glasses   a tambourine

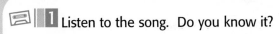

**4** Listen to verse 4 again. Find the words which have an /iː/ sound. *ease*

**5** In the song, The Beatles want to live in a Yellow Submarine. What's your favourite fantasy place?

## Grammar

Present simple –
  frequency adverbs
Object pronouns

## Vocabulary

Free time activities
Rooms

## Communication

Introduce people
Ask about free time

## Listening

**1** Check these words.

practise (v)   sitting room
band   practice (n)   rude

**2** Listen and answer the questions.

1  Is Dave friendly or unfriendly?
2  What time is band practice?

## Reading

| | |
|---|---|
| **Tom** | Isabel! It's late! Why are you still here? |
| **Isabel** | I often stay at school and practise. My piano's in the sitting room at home. |
| **Tom** | Is that a problem? |
| **Isabel** | It's noisy. My brothers always watch TV in the afternoon. |
| **Tom** | Oh, right. This is my friend, Dave. |
| **Isabel** | Hi! Do you play the drums? |
| **Dave** | Yeah! Real music. |
| **Isabel** | Pardon? I play 'real' music too. |
| **Dave** | Classical music! I hate it! It's music for old people! |
| **Isabel** | Hey! |
| **Tom** | Isabel, do you ever play rock? |
| **Isabel** | Yes – I sometimes play Latin or Rock and Roll. |

*(Isabel plays some music.)*

| | |
|---|---|
| **Tom** | Wow! Fantastic! |
| **Dave** | Let's go, Tom. |
| **Tom** | Isabel, do you want to come to band practice? I've got a piano. |
| **Dave** | Tom, are you crazy? She plays Beethoven! |
| **Isabel** | You're rude! What time does it start, Tom? |
| **Tom** | Half past six, at my house. |
| **Isabel** | Good! See you there. |
| **Dave** | Oh, no! |

**3 Read and answer true or false.**

1 Isabel's piano is in her bedroom. ✗
2 Her brothers watch TV in the afternoon.
3 Dave likes classical music.
4 Isabel only plays classical music.
5 Isabel thinks Dave is unfriendly.

**4 Look at the photo below and answer the question.**

1 Who's the man in the photo below?

## Roleplay – Introduce people

**5 Listen and complete the conversation.**

| | |
|---|---|
| **Tom** | ¹ *Hi,* dad! |
| **Mr Adamski** | ² … Tom. |
| **Tom** | Dad, ³ … is Isabel. |
| **Isabel** | ⁴ … do you do, Mr Adamski? |
| **Mr Adamski** | ⁵ … to meet you, Isabel. |

**6 In groups of 3, practise the conversation.**

**7 Look at the pictures and decide which situations are formal/informal.**

①

*Valerie, Pete, Mrs Porter*

②

*Valerie, Pete, Luke*

③

*Mr Jones, Ms Howard, Mr Lewis*

**8 Match these phrases to the situations. Then, listen and check your answers.**

- Hi!/Hello! *[informal]*
- Hello, nice/pleased to meet you. *[formal]*
- How do you do? *[very formal]*

**9 In groups of 3, take it in turns to introduce these people.**

- your teacher to your friend
- your best friend to your mum
- your mum to your boyfriend/girlfriend
- your brother/sister to your friend

# FOCUS 2   Vocabulary – Free time activities

**1** Match the activities to the correct pictures below. Which 6 activities are not in the pictures?

- clean my room ①
- do homework
- go shopping
- go swimming
- go to the cinema
- do Tae Kwon Do
- read a magazine
- run
- text a friend
- play computer games
- play football
- play the piano
- listen to music
- watch TV
- go to a club
- meet friends
- cook
- ride a bike

**Remember**

play football
play computer games
play the piano

_page 2_

There's a girl here called Mel - I really like her. We often do Tae Kwon Do together after school and then we usually go to a café and meet friends.

We sometimes go to Tom's house and listen to music. Tom's in a band with a boy called Dave. (I don't like him, he's always rude and unfriendly.)

Tom's dad is in a wheelchair and Tom usually helps him in the afternoon. Tom goes shopping and he often cooks, but he _is_ human - he never cleans his room!

See you soon!

Love, Isabel x

## Reading

**2** Read the page from Isabel's letter and answer the questions.

1. Does Isabel like Mel?
2. Where does Isabel go after school?
3. Does she like Dave?
4. Why does Tom help his dad?

**3** Which activities from exercise 1 does Isabel write about in her letter?

## Pronunciation – /ə/

**4** Listen and find the /ə/ sound in these words.

| computer | father | human | under |
| thousand | cupboard | woman | after |

_comput**e**r_

**5** Listen again and repeat the words from exercise 4.

**Memory Gym 8**

Free time activities

Go to page 119 ▷▷▷▷

# FOCUS 3  Grammar – Frequency adverbs, Object pronouns

## Frequency adverbs

| | | |
|---|---|---|
| He **never** cleans his room. | 0% ▬▬▬▬▬▬ 100% | |
| We **sometimes** go to Tom's house. | 0% ▬▬▬▬▬▬ 100% | |
| He **often** cooks. | 0% ▬▬▬▬▬▬ 100% | |
| We **usually** go to a café. | 0% ▬▬▬▬▬▬ 100% | |
| He's **always** unfriendly. | 0% ▬▬▬▬▬▬ 100% | |

### Think about language

**Make rules.**

• *He **often** cooks.*
Frequency adverbs go <u>before/after</u> the main verb.

• *He's **always** unfriendly.*
Frequency adverbs go <u>before/after</u> the verb *to be*.

**1** Put the adverbs in the correct place in the sentences.

1  We go to the cinema. (often)

*We often go to the cinema.*

2  They go home at four o'clock. (usually)
3  She's friendly. (always)
4  My father cooks. (never)
5  My uncle is late. (often)
6  I watch TV in the evening. (usually)
7  She goes to a café. (never)

## Speaking

**2** How often do you do these things? In pairs, tell your partner.

1  do your homework at five o'clock in the afternoon

A: How often do you … ?
B: I never do my homework at … .

2  clean your room
3  go shopping with your friends
4  cook the dinner
5  get up at six o'clock
6  have breakfast with your family

| Subject pronouns | Object pronouns |
|---|---|
| I | me |
| you | you |
| he | him |
| she | her |
| it | it |
| we | us |
| they | them |

**3** Replace the nouns in brackets with the correct object pronouns.

1  I don't like (Dave). *I don't like him*.
2  I often go to the gym with (Mel).
3  Do you know (Mickey and his sister)?
4  **Mel:** Can you help (Mel), please?
5  Tom helps (his dad) in the afternoon.
6  **Tom's dad:** Pleased to meet (Isabel), Isabel.
7  Do you like classical music? I hate (classical music).
8  **Tom:** Do you want to play music with (Tom and Dave)?

**4** In pairs, match the names to the photos and talk about the people.

The Beatles   Coldplay   Justin Timberlake
Kylie Minogue   Kurt Cobain   Mary J Blige

A: Who are they?
B: The Beatles.
A: Do you like them?
B: Yes, I do./No, I don't./I don't know them.

55

**1** In pairs, ask questions from the questionnaire. Complete the form for your partner.

**A:** How often do you play football?
Never? Once a week? Sometimes? Or more?
**B:** More. I play football three times a week.

**2** In groups, check the key and talk about your partner.

*Mark plays football once a week ...*

**Remember**
I never play football.
I play football once a week.
twice a week.
three times a week.

*How often do you play football?*

# Are you a
# FITNESS FREAK
## or a
# COUCH POTATO?

## Answer our questionnaire and find out!

## How often do you ...

**1 play football (or other sport)?**
a) never (What's sport?!)   c) once a week
b) sometimes   d) more

**2 run?**
a) never   c) once a week
b) sometimes   d) more

**3 walk a kilometre?**
a) never   c) often
b) sometimes   d) everyday

**4 go swimming?**
a) never (Yuk! A swimming hat?!) c) once a week
b) sometimes   d) more

**5 go to a club?**
a) never   c) once a week
b) sometimes   d) more

**6 watch TV?**
a) never (TV's boring)   c) once a week
b) sometimes   d) every night

**7 watch a video/DVD?**
a) never   c) once a week
b) sometimes   d) more

**8 listen to music?**
a) never   c) often (and loud!)
b) sometimes   d) every day

**9 text a friend?**
a) never   c) often
b) sometimes (I luv texting) d) every day

**10 read a magazine?**
a) never   c) once a week
b) sometimes   d) more

**KEY**

**Questions 1–5**
a: 1   b: 2   c: 3   d: 4

**Questions 5–10**
a: 4   b: 3   c: 2   d: 1

**27–40 = Super fit. See you at the Olympics!**
**14–26 = Not bad. You can do more. Buy a swimming hat!**
**0–13 = Oh dear! You are a couch potato. The only exercise you get is when you switch off the TV!**

# FOCUS 5  Vocabulary – Rooms

**1** Match the words to the correct pictures.

*1 sitting room*

| | | |
|---|---|---|
| sitting room | dining room | hall |
| bedroom | kitchen | bathroom |

**2** Complete the sentences.

1  We cook in the k *i t c h e n* .
2  My bed's in the b _ _ _ _ _ _ .
3  I watch TV in the s _ _ _ _ _ _ r _ _ _ .
4  I have dinner in the d _ _ _ _ _ r _ _ _ .
5  There's a bath in the b _ _ _ _ _ _ _ .
6  The h _ _ _ is behind the front door of
   your house.

## Memory Tip 5

**Think in pictures.**

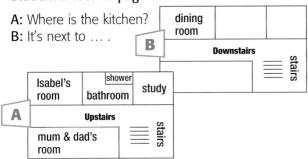

**3** Close your eyes. Visualise your home and
answer the questions. Then ask your partner.

1  How many rooms are there?
2  How many doors are there?
3  Walk through your home and name each room.

*In my house there are …*

## Find out!

**4** Complete the map of Isabel's house.
Student A look at this page. Complete map B.
Student B look at page 135.

A: Where is the kitchen?
B: It's next to … .

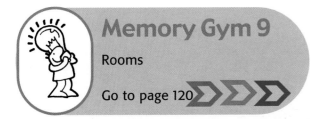

## Memory Gym 9

Rooms

Go to page 120 ▷▷▷▷▷

# FOCUS 6    Skills – East meets West

## Reading

**1** Quick Read. Read the text quickly. How many schools are in the e-mail experiment?

**2** Find these words and check what they mean.

> East    West    exchange    popular
> successful    plans    future

**3** Detailed Read. Read again and answer the questions.

1 What kind of project is it?  *an Internet project*
2 When do Japanese students start school?
3 When do they finish school?
4 How do they usually go to school?
5 Who goes to school five days a week?
6 What do Japanese students do in their free time?
7 Who does homework for two or three hours a night?
8 What do the British students want to do in the future?

## Listening

**4** Listen to Alan talking about his house. Where do these people do their homework?

1 Alan  *in the kitchen*
2 Tony
3 Gill
4 Paula

**5** Listen again. Complete the sentences.

1 There are  *three*  bedrooms in our house.
2 We haven't got a … .
3 Gill is always in the … .
4 We eat in the … .
5 We …… in the sitting room.
6 There's a radio in the … .

## Study skills - Speaking

**Get ready**

When you speak in English, it's difficult to think of good ideas and work out the language at the same time.

Durrrrrrr…

- Before you have a conversation think about your ideas.
- Prepare some words and phrases.

Steve
fourteen
I like …

Hi, my name's Steve. I'm fourteen. I like …

## Speaking

**6** In pairs, talk about your school and free time. Think about the study skill. Prepare your answers.

- When do you go to school?
- What do you do after school?
- Do you do a lot of homework?
- What do you do in your free time?
- one other question

## Writing Gym 5

An article about your school

Go to page 128

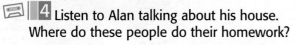

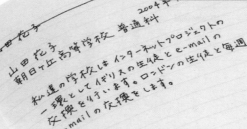

Japanese and British children find out about school life using the Internet. **Joe Reid** reports.

# East meets West

'IT'S a great idea!' says thirteen-year-old Masahiro Suzukawa. She is talking about an e-mail exchange between students at Wakeford school in Britain and Number Three school in Sakata, Japan. The e-mails are part of a new Internet project. Students at 180 British and Japanese schools write and exchange e-mails. The students ask a lot of questions and the answers are always interesting!

## When do you go to school?

Japanese students go to school from 8am to 3pm, six days a week. They always walk or ride bikes. In Britain, school usually starts at 9am and finishes at 4pm. British students go to school five days a week and a lot of them go by car.

In Japan, students clean the school after lessons.

## What do you do after school?

After school in Britain, students meet friends, play computer games or listen to music. They sometimes do homework together. In Japan, students clean the school after their lessons! Then they go to clubs or practise sports. Football and kendo are very popular.

## Do you do a lot of homework?

Japanese students do a lot of homework and they sometimes go to homework schools on Saturday. In Britain, ten-year-olds do half an hour a night. Sixteen-year-olds do two or three hours a night. They usually do their homework at home.

The project is very successful. What are the plans for the future? The British students want to visit their friends in Japan of course!

Sports lesson – this is a Japanese sport called Kendo.

# Energy Check

## Grammar

**1** Find the adverbs and match the sentences to the correct bars.

1 I never walk to school. (a)
2 They usually go shopping in the afternoon.
3 We often get up at six o'clock.
4 She always does her homwork.
5 You sometimes go to the café.

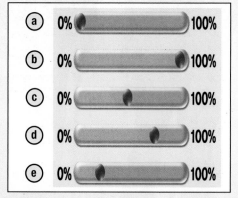

**2** Put the sentences into the correct order.

1 never/they/cook/.

*They never cook.*

2 often/'s/she/late/.
3 usually/watch/TV/in the evening/I/.
4 in the afternoon/'s/she/often/at school/.
5 once a week/play/football/I/.
6 Tae Kwon Do/we/after school/sometimes/do/.
7 at the café/they/are/at this time/usually/.
8 to the cinema/we/go/twice a week/.

**3** Choose the correct words.

1 She doesn't like I/me.
2 We/Us live in this house.
3 They're my parents. They/Them are from France.
4 Do you want to play football with we/us?
5 I don't know. Ask he/him.
6 Don't talk to she/her.

## Vocabulary

**4** Complete the activities with the correct verbs.

1 *do* Tae Kwon Do
2 ... to a club
3 ... the piano
4 ... my homework
5 ... to the cinema
6 ... a magazine
7 ... swimming
8 ... TV
9 ... shopping
10 ... my room
11 ... a bike
12 ... to music

**5** Where do you do these things? Complete the crossword and find the mystery room.

1 You watch TV in this room.
2 There's food in this room.
3 Your bed is in here.
4 A small room behind the front door.
5 There's a bath in this room.

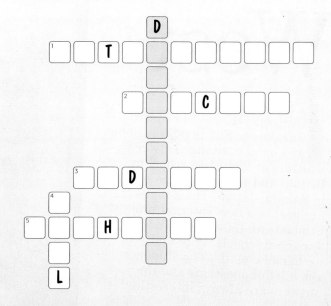

## Communication

**6** Complete the conversation with the correct words.

- How are you?
- Pleased to meet you.
- How do you do?
- Hi!/Hello!
- Nice to meet you.

Luke    ¹ *Hi!* Mum.
Mum    Hi! Luke.
Luke    Mum, this is Pete.
Mum    ²... Pete! ³...... .
Pete    Hello! ⁴... Mrs Young?
Luke    And this is my brother, Mark.
Mark    Hi! ⁵... ?
Pete    Hi! Fine thanks.

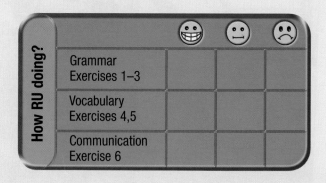

| How RU doing? | 😁 | 😐 | 🙁 |
|---|---|---|---|
| Grammar Exercises 1–3 | | | |
| Vocabulary Exercises 4,5 | | | |
| Communication Exercise 6 | | | |

**1** I'm Ben and I live in a terraced house in West London. There's a small garden but it's noisy because it's near Heathrow airport. Downstairs there is a kitchen, a sitting room and a dining room. There are three bedrooms upstairs and a bathroom. All the houses in our street are the same.

**2** I'm lucky – I've got my sister's old bedroom and it's nice and big. She's eighteen and she's a student in Newcastle now. She lives in a flat with her friends.

**3** My grandparents live near us in a small bungalow with one bedroom. I sometimes help them with their garden and they give me a bit of cash.

I live here!

My grandparents' bungalow

cash = money

## Culture FiLe

**In Britain**

- Most families live in houses – terraced, semi-detached or detached houses.

- 12% of families live in flats.

- 80% of new houses have got 3 or more bedrooms.

- Students often leave home at eighteen. They go to university in another city.

## QUESTiONS

**1** Read about Ben and answer the questions.

1 What type of home does Ben live in?
2 How many bedrooms are there?
3 Where does Ben's sister live?
4 What type of home do his grandparents live in?

**2** In groups, discuss the questions

1 What kind of homes are there in your country?
2 How many bedrooms are there in your friends' houses?
3 When do people usually leave home in your country?

**Grammar**
can/can't (ability)
Imperatives

**Vocabulary**
Adjectives
Parts of the body

**Communication**
Make suggestions
Talk about abilities

**FOCUS 1** Switch On

## Listening

**1** Check these words.

| sing   voice   quiet   shout |
| singer   song   microphone |

**2** Listen and answer the questions.

1 Who is a good singer?
2 Who is a bad singer?

62

## Reading

| | |
|---|---|
| Tom | 'Come on baby light my fire ...' |
| Dave | Aaargh! Tom, you can't sing! We play rock music, not folk! |
| Mel | Don't shout, Dave. You've got a nice voice, Tom, but it's a bit quiet. |
| Tom | Great! Thanks a lot! |
| Mickey | Hi, guys. Good band practice? |
| Dave | No, it's terrible. We need a singer. |
| Mickey | What's the song? |
| Isabel | *Light my fire.* |
| Mickey | 'Come on baby light my fire ...' |
| Tom | Not bad, Mickey. Can you sing with a microphone? OK, sing it again. |
| Mickey | 'Come on baby light my fire ...' |
| Dave | That's great, Mickey! |
| Tom | What do you think, Mel? |
| Mel | Well, he can sing, he can dance and he's good-looking. |
| Dave | Oh, no! Now it's a pop band! |
| Tom | Mickey, do you want to join our band? |
| Isabel | Mmm. That's a good idea! |
| Mickey | Umm ... I'm not sure. |
| Mel | Let's go to the café and talk about it. |
| Tom | Good thinking! |

**3** Choose the correct words.

1 Dave likes/doesn't like Tom's voice.
2 The band plays folk/rock music.
3 Dave likes/doesn't like Mickey's voice.
4 Mel thinks Mickey is good/bad for the band.
5 Isabel wants/doesn't want Mickey in the band.

**4** Complete the phrases from the conversation. Then check what they mean.

1 T h a n k s a lot!
2 Hi, _ _ _ _ .
3 N _ _ b _ _ .
4 I'm not s _ _ _ .
5 G _ _ _ thinking!

## Vocabulary – Adjectives

**5** Match the adjectives to the correct pictures. Then listen and check.

| great | clean | loud | interesting | dirty | quiet |
|---|---|---|---|---|---|
| modern | old-fashioned | terrible | boring | | |

*1 great*

## Roleplay – Make suggestions

**6** Listen and complete.

1 Mel   Let's go to a ¹*café*.
  Tom   ²... thinking!
  Dave  That's a ³... idea.
2 Dave  Do you ⁴... to watch TV?
  Mel   No, that's a ⁵... idea.
  Tom   I think that's a ⁶... idea.

**7** Your teacher is late. In groups, make suggestions for the situations and decide what to do.

- go home
- listen to a CD
- do our homework
- go to a café
- tidy the classroom
- practise our English!
- sing a song
- *your ideas*

A: Let's go home.
B: That's a good idea.
C: That's a boring idea. Let's ...

**Memory Gym 10**

Adjectives

Go to page 120 ⟫⟫⟫

# FOCUS 2   Grammar – *can/can't* (ability)

| Positive | Negative | Questions | Short answers |
|---|---|---|---|
| I/You<br>He/She/It } can sing.<br>We/They | I/You<br>He/She/It } can't sing.<br>We/They | Can { I/you<br>he/she/it<br>we/they } sing? | Yes, I can./No, I can't.<br>Yes, you can./No, you can't. |
| *Mickey can sing.* | *Tom can't sing.* | *Can you sing?* | **Wh-** questions |
| | | | *What can they do?*<br>*Who can dance?* |

## Think about language

**Make a rule.**

***can/can't*** are the same/different after all
Subject pronouns.

WEDNESDAY 9 APRIL 2003   MEL

Great! We've got a singer for the
band – Mickey Kelly!

Tom isn't happy because Mickey is VERY
cute and Isabel likes him!!

Tom's a really good musician. He can play
the guitar, he can read music and he
writes great songs, but he can't sing
or dance.

Mickey can sing, he can dance and he can
play the guitar a bit. He can't read music
but he's very confident.

Problems in the future? Maybe ...

**1** Read Mel's diary and answer true or false.

1  Tom can play the guitar. ✓
2  Tom can write songs.
3  Tom can dance.
4  Mickey can sing.
5  Mickey can play the guitar.
6  Mickey can read music.

## Pronunciation – /ə/, /æ/, /ɑ:/

**2** Listen to the pronunciation of *can* and *can't*.

a) /ə/ He c<u>a</u>n sing.     Who c<u>a</u>n dance?
b) /æ/ Yes, we c<u>a</u>n.     Yes they c<u>a</u>n.
c) /ɑ:/ They c<u>a</u>n't sing.   No, I c<u>a</u>n't.

**3** Listen to *can* in the sentences. Is it a, b or c? Then
listen again and repeat.

1  Who c<u>a</u>n play the guitar? *a*
2  Mel c<u>a</u>n't sing.
3  Yes, he c<u>a</u>n.
4  She c<u>a</u>n play the piano.
5  Yes, I c<u>a</u>n.
6  I c<u>a</u>n't read music.

**4** Write about Mickey and Tom.

| sing   dance   write songs<br>read music   play the guitar |
|---|

*Mickey can sing but Tom can't.*

## Find out!

**5** Student A look at this page.
Student B go to page 135. Ask and
answer. What can Keanu Reeves do?

A: Can he sing?
B: No, he can't./Yes, he can.

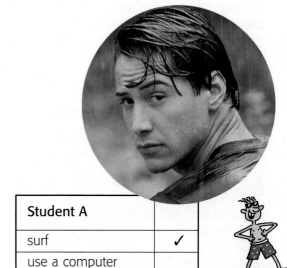

| Student A | |
|---|---|
| surf | ✓ |
| use a computer | |
| speak Spanish | |
| speak Japanese | ✗ |
| sing | ✓ |
| dance | |
| play the guitar | |
| run 1 kilometre | ✓ |
| swim | |
| write songs | ✓ |
| read music | ✓ |
| play the piano | |

# Melton International Children's Camp

## Holiday job ability checklist

| | Yes [✓] | Job A | Job B | Job C |
|---|---|---|---|---|
| use a computer | ✓ | ● | | |
| type | ✓ | ● | | |
| swim | ✓ | | | ● |
| speak English | ✓ | ● | ● | ● |
| speak two other languages | ✓ | ● | ● | ● |
| sing | ✗ | ● | ● | |
| run 1 km | ✓ | | | ● |
| play volleyball | ✓ | | | ● |
| play the piano | ✗ | | ● | ● |
| play the guitar | ✗ | | ● | ● |
| play chess | ✗ | | | ● |
| draw | ✗ | ● | ● | |
| dance | ✓ | | ● | |
| stand on your hands | ✓ | | ● | |

**1** You have got an interview at Melton Children's Camp for a holiday job. First, check the activities.

**2** Student A you are the camp organiser. Ask student B the questions and complete the table for him/her. Student B answer the questions.

**A:** Can you use a computer?
**B:** Yes, I can./No, I can't.

**3** Do the interview again. Student A answer the questions. Student B you are the organiser.

**4** Now look at the key and count the coloured dots. What job can your partner do?

## Writing

**5** Write a report about your partner's job.

*I think the right job for … is a/an … because he/she can … but he/she can't …*

**Key**
Which colours?
Mainly ● = Job A an office assistant.
Mainly ● = Job B an entertainer
Mainly ● = Job C a sports and games assistant

65

# FOCUS 4   Vocabulary – Parts of the body

There are twenty-seven bones and thirty-seven muscles in your hand. About half of your bones are in your hands and feet.

Hair grows about one centimetre a month. It's very slow!

There are 206 bones in your body, but there are 270 bones in a baby's body.

There are forty muscles in your face. You use twenty-five muscles when you smile!

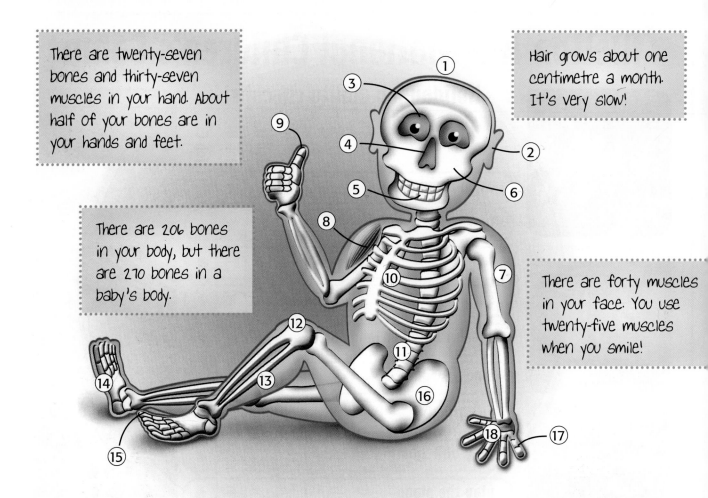

**1** Read the texts above and answer true or false.

1  You have got 200 bones in your body. ✗
2  There are thirty-seven muscles in your hand.
3  Half of your bones are in your feet.
4  You use forty muscles when you smile.
5  Hair grows forty centimetres a month.

**2** Match the words to the correct parts of the body.

| head   arm   leg   nose   hand |
| foot/feet   ear   finger   toe   mouth |
| thumb   knee   eyes   stomach |
| face   chest   bone   muscle |

*1  head*

## Memory Tip 6

**Draw pictures to remember.**
Some people remember pictures better than words.

• Draw pictures of new words and label them in English.

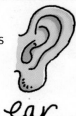

*ear*

**3** In pairs, cover exercise 2 and check your partner.

A: What's number 1 … ?
B: It's his head.

### Remember

hair and feet
• we say hair not hairs
• the plural of foot is feet

**Memory Gym 11**

Parts of the body

Go to page 121 ⟩⟩⟩

# FOCUS 5   Grammar – Imperatives

| Positive | | Negative | |
|---|---|---|---|
| *Sing it again.* | *Stand on the right.* | *Don't shout.* | *Do not smoke.* |

### Think about language

**Make rules.**
* To make a negative imperative use … before the verb.
* The long form of **don't** is … .

**1** Complete the instructions for each picture.

1 Move your ..*ears*.. but don't move your … .

4 Close your … and touch your … with your … .

2 Touch your … .

5 Close your … and touch two … .

3 Close one … .

6 Do this with your … .

**2** In pairs, can you do the instructions?

**3** Match the instructions to the correct signs.

1 Do not use mobile phones. (e)
2 Please stand on the right.
3 Do not drink the water.
4 Do not play ball games.
5 Put your rubbish in the wastebin.
6 Please do not smoke.

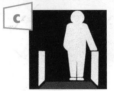 

### Listening

**4** Listen and match the conversations to the correct signs from exercise 3.

*1 e*

**5** Write 3 positive and 3 negative instructions. Use these verbs. Then tell your partner what to do.

| close | move | touch |
|---|---|---|
| do | stand (up) | sit |

A: Close your eyes and …

# Here's Koko

A   This is a photo of Koko with her friend the scientist, Dr Francine Patterson. Koko is a gorilla. She lives in Miami and she likes dolls and cats.

B   Koko and Dr Patterson are part of the Gorilla Language Project. Dr Patterson wants to answer the question: 'Can gorillas talk to people?' She is Koko's teacher.

C   Koko can't speak but she can make signs with her hands. She uses a sign language for people who can't hear or speak. Koko can use 1,000 signs. She can say 'drink', 'apple', 'cat', 'hungry' and 'love', for example. Dr Patterson makes signs and talks to Koko too. Koko can understand 2,000 words and signs. Koko can't type but sometimes she chats on a website. Dr Patterson translates Koko's signs and types them onto the website for her.

D   Koko isn't human, but she is intelligent and has got feelings. She can smile and laugh. She can also remember things for many years. Can gorillas really talk to people? Koko can.

www.koko.org

## FOCUS 6   Skills – Can gorillas talk to people?

### Study skills – Reading

**Look for paragraphs**
- Paragraphs break texts into sections.
- Each paragraph usually has a new idea.

Koko is a gorilla. She lives in Miami and she likes dolls and cats. Koko and Dr Patterson are part of the Gorilla Language Project. Dr Patterson wants to answer the question: 'Can gorillas talk to people?' She is Koko's teacher. Koko can't speak but she can make signs with her hands. She uses a sign language for people who can't hear or speak. Koko can use 1,000 signs.

← difficult to understand

Koko is a gorilla. She lives in Miami and she likes dolls and cats.

Koko and Dr Patterson are part of the Gorilla Language Project. Dr Patterson wants to answer the question: 'Can gorillas talk to people?' She is Koko's teacher.

Koko can't speak but she can make signs with her hands. She uses a sign language for people who can't hear or speak. Koko can use 1,000 signs.

← easy to understand

### Reading

**1** Quick Read. Think about the study skill. Match the paragraphs in the article about Koko to the correct ideas.

1  Things Koko can and can't do.  (c)
2  Who is Koko?
3  The Gorilla Language Project.
4  Koko's human qualities.

**2** Detailed Read. Answer the questions.

1  Who is Francine Patterson?
2  Where does Koko live?
3  Why are they together?
4  Can Koko speak?
5  Who usually uses sign language?
6  Does Dr Patterson talk to Koko?
7  Can Koko type?
8  Can she remember things?

**3** Complete the sentences with information from the article.

*Koko can … . She can't … .*

Koko with her cat, 'Lips Lipstick' and Dr Patterson.

Baby Koko with her friend, the scientist Dr Francine Patterson.

## Speaking

**4** In pairs, talk about what Koko's signs mean.

*I think number 1 means … ./I don't know.*

## Listening

**5** Listen and check your answers from exercise 4.

a) cat
b) me
c) drink  ①
d) time
e) tickle

**6** Listen again and write the instructions for each sign.

*Touch your …*

### Writing Gym 6

A description of an animal

Go to page 129

# Energy Check

## Grammar

**1** Complete the sentences with *can* or *can't*.

(✔ = can ✗ = can't)

|  | Dennis | Liz |
|---|---|---|
| sing | ✗ | ✔ |
| dance | ✗ | ✔ |
| read music | ✔ | ✗ |

1 Dennis *can't* sing.
2 Liz … sing.
3 Liz … dance.
4 Dennis … read music.
5 Dennis … dance.
6 Liz … read music.

**2** Make questions with *can*. Then answer the questions.

1 you/swim?

*Can you swim? Yes, I can.*

2 Koko/laugh?
3 Tom/sing?
4 you/play the piano?
5 your parents/play chess?
6 your sister/use a mobile phone?
7 you/stand on your hands?
8 your teacher/dance?

**3** Make instructions for your classroom. Use positive or negative imperatives.

1 (stand) on the desk

*Don't stand on the desk.*

2 (sit) on your chair
3 (put) your rubbish in the wastebin
4 (play) football in class
5 (use) mobile phones in class
6 (do) your homework

## Vocabulary

**4** Label the parts of the body. *1 Head*

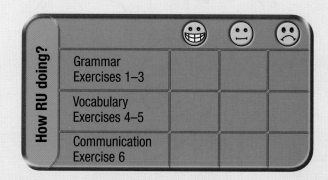

**5** Complete with the opposite of the underlined adjectives.

1 This lesson isn't <u>interesting</u> it's *boring*.
2 My room isn't <u>dirty</u>, it's … .
3 Her car isn't <u>modern</u>, it's … .
4 Mickey's voice isn't <u>terrible</u>, it's … .
5 I don't like <u>quiet</u> music, I like … music.

## Communication

**6** Make responses to the suggestions.

1 Let's go to the cinema! (✔)

*That's a good idea.*

2 Let's do our homework! (✗)
3 Do you want to play football? (✔)
4 Do you want to watch TV? (✗)

| How RU doing? | | 😁 | 😐 | 😟 |
|---|---|---|---|---|
| | Grammar Exercises 1–3 | | | |
| | Vocabulary Exercises 4–5 | | | |
| | Communication Exercise 6 | | | |

# Mambo Number 5

"One, two, three, four, five,

everybody in the car so come on let's ride ..."

Mambo Number 5 is a hit from 1999 for the singer Lou Bega. Is he from New York? Cuba? No, he comes from ... Belgium!

'Mambo' is a dance.
It comes from Cuba.
Mambo dancers are called 'Mambonics'.

**1** Listen to the song. Is it pop or rock?

**2** Think about these questions:

a Do you know the song?
b Is it happy or sad?
c Is it a good song for dancing?

**3** Listen to the chorus and match the sentences.

a little bit of Monica — all night long
a little bit of Erica — in the sun
a little bit of Rita — here I am
a little bit of Tina — in my life
a little bit of Sandra — by my side
a little bit of Mary — all I need
a little bit of Jessica — is what I see
a little bit of you — makes me your man

**4** This part of the song is a dance. Put the verbs in the correct place.

| take | shake | put | move |
|------|-------|-----|------|
| jump | clap | clap | |

And 1 ...... up and down
and 2 ...... it all around
3 ...... your head to the sound
4 ...... your hand on the ground
5 ...... one step left
And one step right
One to the front
And one to the side
6 ...... your hands once
And 7 ...... your hands twice
And if it looks like this
Then you're doin' it right.

**5** Now, listen again and check.

**6** Listen again. Can you do this dance?

71

# Projects

# My life as a Pizza!

## Project 1  A recipe of your life.

1 Copy the time sheet below.

2 Keep the time sheet with you for 24 hours on a normal school day. Write everything you do on that day in the correct place on the time sheet. Complete it every 30 minutes. (OK, not when you're asleep or in maths!)

**Possible activities**

sleep  wash  help at home  study

other activities  play sport/do exercise

eat

watch TV/listen to the radio

travel  do homework

### Time Sheet

| Time | Activity |
|------|----------|
| 6:00 am | |
| 6:30 | |
| 7:00 | eat breakfast |
| 7:30 | |
| 8:00 | |
| 8:30 | |
| 9:00 | |
| 9:30 | |
| 10:00 | |
| 10:30 | |
| 11:00 | |
| 11:30 | |
| 12:00 pm | |

# Project 2  Make a pizza-graph.

**1** Study the results on your time sheet. How much time do you spend on each activity?

**2** Read the recipe and make your own pizza.

## Pizza-graph of My Day

## Recipe - My Day

Preparation time  1 hour
Serves            1 person
Ingredients       pens, pencils, magazines, scissors, glue

Method
1) draw the pizza and colour each slice with a different colour
2) find pictures in magazines and cut them out
3) stick your pictures onto your pizza
put your pizza-graph on your classroom wall

Eat the pizza

- 🌿 **Eat**
- 🌿 **School**
- 🌿 **Travel**
- 🌿 **Homework**
- 🌿 **Other**
- 🌿 **Sleep**
- 🌿 **TV**
- 🌿 **On the phone**

**Grammar**
Present continuous

**Vocabulary**
Money
Music

**Communication**
Describe a scene
Buy things

**FOCUS 1    Switch on**

## Listening

**1 Check these words.**

stage    buy    tickets    queue    joke    wait for

**2 Listen and answer the questions.**

1  Where are Mel and Isabel?
2  Where are Tom and Dave?

## Reading

**Mel**  Hi, Tom!

**Tom**  Mel! What's up? What are you doing?

**Mel**  I'm with Isabel. We're waiting for Mickey.

**Tom**  So he's late again! The band's coming on stage now!

**Mel**  I know. I can hear them.

**Tom**  Where are you?

**Mel**  We're buying tickets. We're waiting in a queue at the moment but it isn't moving. How much are the tickets?

**Tom**  Seven pounds fifty each.

**Mel**  What!?! You're joking!

**Tom**  But four pounds with a student ID.

**Mel**  Oh, good! Are you standing near the stage, Tom?

**Tom**  Yes, we are. We're in front of the stage, on the right.

# Hellooo!!

**Mel**  Ouch! Who's shouting?

**Tom**  Sorry, it's Dave. He's saying hello!

**Mel**  Muppet! Hey, I can see Mickey! See you later.

**3** Read the conversation and correct the sentences.

1 Mel is with Mickey. *Mel is with Isabel.*
2 Tom is late.
3 The tickets are seven pounds fifty each.
4 Tom's in front of the stage, on the left.
5 Mel can see Dave.

**4** Complete the phrases from the conversation. Then check what they mean.

1 What's u _?
2 W _ _ _ !?!
3 You're j _ _ _ _ _ !
4 See you l _ _ _ _ .

## Vocabulary – Money

> ### Remember
> The signs go before the numbers.
>
> £20 twenty pounds
> £20.50 twenty pounds fifty p(ence)

**5** Say these prices. Then listen and check.

| | | | |
|---|---|---|---|
| 1 | £1.00 | 5 | £2.99 |
| 2 | £1.50 | 6 | £1.60 |
| 3 | £15.00 | 7 | £13.74 |
| 4 | £80.00 | 8 | £20.00 |

**6** In pairs, match the prices to the correct objects.

£1.20   £2.80   £79.99   £1.00   £13.75

**A:** How much is the … ?
**B:** I think it's … .

**7** Listen and check. Compare the prices with your answers from exercise 6.

1 the bottle of cola   *£1.00*
2 the hamburger
3 the mobile phone
4 the bus ticket
5 the CD

# FOCUS 2 Grammar – Present continuous

| Positive | Negative | Questions | Short answers |
|---|---|---|---|
| I'm<br>You're<br>He's/She's/It's<br>We're/They're } singing. | I'm not<br>You aren't<br>He/She/It isn't<br>We/They aren't } singing. | Am I<br>Are you<br>Is he/she<br>Are we/they } singing? | Yes, I am./No, I'm not.<br>Yes, you are./No, you aren't. |
| *I'm waiting in a queue at the moment.* | *I'm not waiting.* | *Are you waiting?* | **Wh- questions**<br>*What are they doing?*<br>*Who is shouting?* |

## Think about language

**Make rules.**
- To make the Present continuous negative put *not* <u>before/after</u> *am*, *is* or *are*.
- To make a Present continuous question put *am*, *is* or *are* <u>before/after</u> the Subject pronoun.

**1** Check these verbs. Then write the *-ing* form. Be careful of the spelling changes.

| sing | *singing* |
|---|---|
| read | |
| cook | |
| study | |
| watch | |
| listen | |
| play | |
| sleep | |
| write | *writing* |
| dance | |
| have | |
| move | |
| come | |
| shop | *shopping* |
| sit | |
| run | |

**2** Complete the phone conversation with the correct form of the present continuous. Use the verbs in brackets.

**Sam** Hi, Helen! What ¹ (do) *are* you *doing* ? ² (play) … you … a computer game?

**Helen** No, I ³ (do) … my homework at the moment. What ⁴ (do) … Sarah … ?

**Sam** She ⁵ (sit) … on my bed and she ⁶ (read) … a magazine. Hey! I can hear music. ⁷ (listen) … you … to a CD?

**Helen** No, I'm not. My brother ⁸ (play) … the guitar – it's very loud!

Remember

drop the final e
writ → writing
       e

76

**3** In pairs, make false sentences about the people in the photos. Correct your partner's sentences. Use these verbs.

| | | | | | | |
|---|---|---|---|---|---|---|
| eat | run | sit | stand | read | sing | dance |
| talk | watch | cry | shop | wait | listen | |

A: He's sleeping.
B: He isn't sleeping. He's reading.

**4** In pairs, student A choose a person in the photos. Student B ask questions. Who is it?

A: Is it a man or a woman?
B: It's a man.
A: Is he sitting in a chair?
B: Yes, he is./No, he isn't.

## Roleplay – Describe a scene

**5** Student A you are at a concert. Student B you are at home. Call your friend on his/her mobile and have a conversation.

A: Hello.
B: Hi! Is that … ?
A: Yes, it is. Hi, … ! Where are you?
B: I'm at home and I'm bored. Where are you? What are you doing?
A: (*Describe where you are and what you are doing.*)
B: What can you see? What are people doing?
A: (*Describe three people from the pictures or invent some people.*)
B: You're lucky! Are you having a good time?
A: …

**6** Now write the conversation.

football shirts £....

posters £....

caps £3.99

dolls £....

bus £....

cameras £....

pencils 80p

postcards 20p

sunglasses £8.75

wallets £6.50   pens £1.15   notebooks ...p

## Reading

| Laura | How much are these pencils? |
|---|---|
| Seller | Eighty p each. |
| Laura | And a cap? |
| Seller | Three pounds ninety-nine. |
| Laura | And wallets? |
| Seller | Wallets are six pounds fifty. |
| Laura | Can I have two postcards, a cap and two pencils, please? |
| Seller | That's six pounds ninety-nine, please. |
| Laura | Here you are. |
| Seller | Great, thanks. |
| Laura | Wait a minute – that isn't right. |

**1** Listen, read and answer the questions.

1  What does Laura buy?
2  How much does the seller ask for?
3  What's the correct price?

## Find out!

**2** Student A look at this page. Student B go to page 136. Complete the prices of the things in the photo.

A: How much is this/that/a cap?
B: It's … .
A: How much are these/those sunglasses?
B: They're … .

**3** Use this photo. Student A you want to buy a present for each person in your family. You've got £15.00. Student B you are the seller.

A: How much is … ?
B: It's … .
A: Can I have a … ?
B: Here you are. That's … .
A: Thank you.

**4** Student B you want to buy a present for each person in your family. You've got £24.00.

# FOCUS 4   Vocabulary – Music

**1** In pairs, look at the photos. What types of music can you find?

*Number 1 is jazz, I think.*

**2** Do you know any other types of music?

**3** Match the types of music to bands you know.

*Rap – Eminem.*

---

## Memory Tip 7

**Think of similar words in your language.**

---

## Pronunciation /ʌ/, /æ/

**4** Listen and repeat these words.

/æ/ jazz classical Latin bag
/ʌ/ punk under country drums

**5** Listen and choose the words you hear.

| | /æ/ | /ʌ/ |
|---|---|---|
| 1 | cap | cup |
| 2 | ran | run |
| 3 | bag | bug |
| 4 | cat | cut |
| 5 | and | under |

## Listening

**6** Listen and decide. What type of music is it?

*1 jazz*

**7** In pairs or groups, talk about the types of music you like and don't like.

A: What type of music do you like?
B: I like pop and rock, but I don't like jazz. And you?

---

## Memory Gym 12

Music

Go to page 121 >>>>

---

# MUSIC ONLINE

**SHOPPING**

**Blues**
**Techno**
**Rap**
**Jazz**
**Country**
**Folk**
**Classical**
**Rock**
**Pop**
**Punk**
**Metal**
**Latin**

**CLICK NOW !**

## Reading

**1** Quick Read. Read the text quickly. What text type is it?

**a)** a form   **b)** an advertisement   **c)** an article

**2** Detailed Read. Read the text again and choose the correct words.

1 Pop Dreams is …
   **a)** a TV programme. **b)** a cassette.   **c)** a video.
2 There are … people watching Pop Dreams on TV.
   **a)** fifty             **b)** 3,000        **c)** millions of
3 Pop Dreams is looking for …
   **a)** dancers.           **b)** David Yates. **c)** singers.
4 … people are invited to sing in front of the judges.
   **a)** fifty             **b)** 3,000        **c)** five million
5 This year's winner is called …
   **a)** Pop Star.        **b)** Pop Dream.  **c)** David Yates.
6 David is in …
   **a)** the theatre.     **b)** Britain.    **c)** Las Vegas.

### Study skills – Dictionary work

**Before you use the dictionary!**

- Examine the word. Is it a noun, an adjective or a verb?

| *Are you a musician?* | **noun** |
| *Have you got a good voice?* | **adjective** |
| *I'm travelling all over the world.* | **verb** |

- Guess the meaning. Look at the context.

*Are you a talented musician?*
a  Is *talented* an adjective, a noun or a verb?
b  Do they want good, very good or bad musicians?
c  What does *talented* mean?

**3** Think about the study skill. Are the underlined words nouns, adjectives or verbs? Can you guess their meaning?

1 3,000 people are sitting in the theatre.
2 Some people can't perform in front of TV cameras.
3 I'm recording a new song in Las Vegas.
4 It isn't easy.
5 You can win too!

## Listening

**4** Listen to 3 contestants from *Pop Dreams*. Complete the table with information about them.

|  | Pattie | Rob | Jane |
|---|---|---|---|
| 1 from? | London |  |  |
| 2 job? |  |  |  |
| 3 boyfriend/girlfriend? |  |  |  |
| 4 favourite band/singer? |  |  |  |
| 5 song today? |  |  |  |

## Speaking

**5** Invent a new contestant for *Pop Dreams* and make notes about him/her. Then in pairs, ask and answer the questions from exercise 4.

A: What's your name and where are you from?
B: I'm … and I'm from … .

**Writing Gym 7**

A form

Go to page 130 ⟫⟫⟫

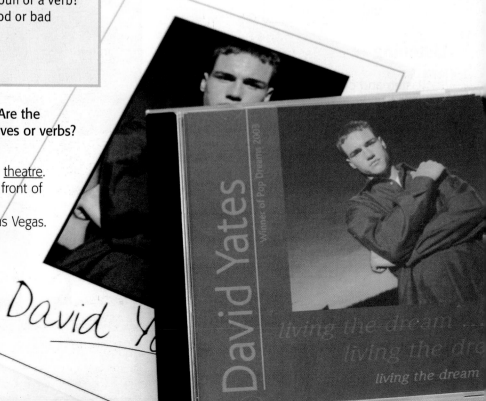

# Do you want to be a Pop star?

You're on stage. 3,000 people are sitting in the theatre in front of you. Millions of people are watching you on TV. Pick up the microphone, open your mouth and start to sing.

Is this you? Do you want to be a pop star?

Pop Dreams is looking for Britain's next number one pop star. Are you a talented musician? Have you got a good voice? We're looking for YOU.

It isn't easy. There are 10,000 people in this competition and they want to be number one too. Some people can't perform in front of TV cameras. Can you sing in front of millions of people? Yes? Contact us today!

## What do you do?

1. Record your favourite song on video or cassette and send it to Pop Dreams.

2. We look at all of your videos and cassettes and invite fifty people to the TV programme.

3. Sing your song in front of our judges and the television cameras. Then the competition starts!

**Write off for an entry form NOW!**

## Pop Dreams

*I'm having a fantastic time! I'm travelling all over the world. My new CD is coming out today and I'm recording a new song in Las Vegas. It's hard work but it's great fun! Try it! You can win too!*

This year's winner – David Yates

**IMPORTANT** If you are under 16 please ask your parent or guardian to fill in this form and bring it along with you to the audition.

Name _____

Address _____

Age _____

Signed _____ (parent or guardian)

Date _____

# Energy Check

## Grammar

**1** Choose the correct words.

1 I **'m**/'s reading a book.
2 She aren't/**isn't** talking to her friend now.
3 The dog 're/**'s** sleeping.
4 Mary and Tom is/**are** coming now.
5 My mother 'm not/**isn't** reading.
6 We **aren't**/isn't sitting in here.

**2** Complete with the correct form of the present continuous. Use the verbs in brackets.

1 A: What (do) *are* you *doing* at the moment?
  B: I (play) … my guitar.
2 A: What (do) … Kim … ?
  B: She (sleep) … .
3 A: (work) … Mary and Tim … now?
  B: No, they (watch TV) … .
4 A: (listen to) … your mother … music?
  B: Yes, she (listen to) … jazz.
5 A: (buy) … you … tickets?
  B: No, I (wait) … for Mickey.

**3** Write the *-ing* form of the verbs.

| | | | | | |
|---|---|---|---|---|---|
| sing | sit | cook | draw | write | use |
| type | read | run | swim | dance | |

*singing, …*

**4** Look at the picture and correct the sentences.

1 He's playing the piano.

*He isn't playing the piano.*
*He's playing a guitar.*

2 She's playing a guitar.
3 She's standing at the piano.
4 They're talking.

## Vocabulary

**5** Find the music words.

1 zazj *jazz*   5 knup
2 lsascliac   6 cork
3 nochet   7 slube
4 trouncy   8 natil

**6** Write the prices.

*1 one pound fifty*

## Communication

**7** Write a conversation for a buyer and a seller in a shop. Use the words and prices from exercise 6.

**Buyer** How much is a can of cola?
**Seller** It's … .
**Buyer** Can I have …, please?

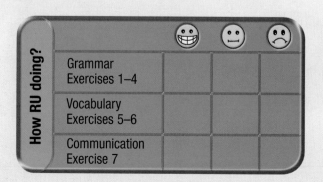

| How RU doing? | | 😁 | 😐 | 😟 |
|---|---|---|---|---|
| | Grammar Exercises 1–4 | | | |
| | Vocabulary Exercises 5–6 | | | |
| | Communication Exercise 7 | | | |

# CULTURE BITE    Music and me

**1** I'm Alex and I'm from Birmingham. I'm into all types of music but at the moment I'm listening to a lot of rock and metal. I love Alien Ant Farm, Nirvana, Iron Maiden, White Stripes. Do you know White Stripes? They are so cool.

White Stripes

**2** I listen to music all the time at home – on CD and the radio. Popular radio stations are 1FM and Kiss. They play pop, rock, rap, dance – everything. I buy a CD every month with the money from my paper round.

**3** I love rock concerts. I sometimes go with my friends. Tickets are between £10 and £20. In the summer I want to go to the Reading Festival – four days of live music – fantastic!

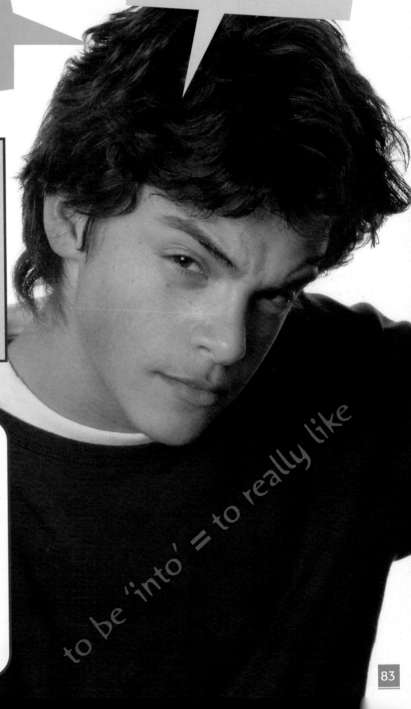

## Culture FiLe

### In Britain

- There are radio stations for all types of music. 1FM and Kiss FM play chart music. Shockin' FM plays Hip Hop and Rap, XFM plays rock.

- CDs cost between £10 and £15.

- Glastonbury and Reading are big rock festivals. Glastonbury costs £75 for the weekend.

## QUESTIONS

**1** Read about Alex and answer the questions.

1  What music does Alex like?
2  How much do concert tickets cost?
3  How many days is the Reading Festival?
4  How much do CDs cost?

**2** In groups, discuss the questions.

1  What music do you like?
2  Do you go to concerts?
3  What's your favourite radio station?

to be 'into' = to really like

**Grammar**
*was/were*
Past simple positive

**Vocabulary**
Days/years/months
Ordinal numbers

**Communication**
Interview a star
Talk about the past

# MY so-LIFE called

- My History
- School
- Home Life
- Interests

## MY HISTORY

My full name is Tomasz Piotr Adamski (but you can call me Tom). I was born in Poland fifteen years ago. My birthday is on 8th June.

My father is Polish and my mother is English. They were musicians in Kraków. We came to England when I was two and lived in London. My dad and I moved to Manchester eleven years ago. My mum stayed in London.

## SCHOOL

My first school was called Moorside Primary. I started there when I was five. I started at Dalesway Secondary when I was eleven. I'm in Year eleven. I go to school from Monday to Friday, nine o'clock to four o'clock. I like Wednesday afternoon because we study my favourite subject – music. We're learning about African music at the moment. School's OK. I've got some great friends.

## HOME LIFE

My home life is a bit unusual because my dad's in a wheelchair. He's cool – he helps me with my music and I help him in the house. On Tuesdays I go shopping. We clean the house on Sundays, so the kitchen and bathroom are clean but my room's a real mess! I usually go out and meet friends on Sunday afternoon.

## INTERESTS

I started a band last year. We usually practise on Saturday afternoon and Thursday evening. My dad's a record producer and he gave us some old equipment. The band's called NRG!

## Reading

**1** Check these words.

| be born | subject | learn |
| unusual | mess | equipment |

**2** Look at the text about Tom. Where is it from?

a) a book  b) an advertisement  c) a webpage

**3** Read the text and complete the table.

| 1 full name | Tom Piotr Adamski |
|---|---|
| 2 date of birth | |
| 3 father's nationality | |
| 4 mother's nationality | |
| 5 first school | |
| 6 school now | |
| 7 information about his mother | |
| 8 information about his father | |
| 9 interests | |

## Vocabulary – Days

**4** Look at the text again and complete the days of the week.

M ➡ *Monday*

| Week 1 | |
|---|---|
| **M** | |
| **T** | |
| **W** | |
| **T** | |
| **F** | |
| **S** | |
| **S** | |
| | |

**5** Listen and check your answers. Then listen again and repeat.

## Speaking

**6** In pairs, ask and answer the questions.

1  What day is it today?

A: What day is it today?
B: It's … .

2  What day is it tomorrow?
3  What day does school start every week?
4  What day does school finish?
5  What's your favourite day? Why?
6  Which days are bad days? Why?

**7** Complete the diary in exercise 4 about Tom's week. Write 1 sentence for each day.

*On Monday Tom goes to school.*

Remember

Monday

on Monday

## Roleplay – Interview a star

**8** Student A you are a reporter. Interview a star about his/her week. Think about questions to ask. Student B you are a star. Decide who you are and write a diary for the week.

**9** Now do the interview together.

A: What do you do on Monday?
B: I usually… then I …

# FOCUS 2 Grammar – *was/were/wasn't/weren't*

| Positive | Negative | Questions | Short answers |
|---|---|---|---|
| I was<br>you were<br>he/she/it was<br>we/they were | I wasn't<br>you weren't<br>he/she/it wasn't<br>we/they weren't | Was I ...?<br>Were you ...?<br>Was he/she/it ...?<br>Were we/they ...? | Yes, I was./No, I wasn't.<br>Yes, you were./No, you weren't. |
| *Our friends were there.* | *You weren't there.* | *Were you there?* | ***Wh-* questions** |
| | | | *Who was there?*<br>*Where were you?* |

### Think about language

**Make *was/were* rules.**
- *I, he/she* and *it* use ... .
- *You*, *we* and *they* use ... .
- To make a negative add ... .

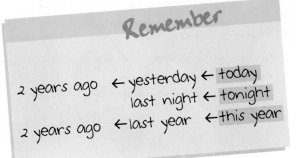

TUESDAY 13 MAY 200...

There was a party at Isabel's house on Saturday night. It was her birthday. The music was great and the food was fantastic. Some of our friends from school were there but Tom wasn't! I texted him but his mobile was off!!! On a Saturday night! He wasn't at home, so where was he? Isabel and Mickey were worried but I was angry. I think Tom was really rude – Isabel's a friend.

**1 Read Mel's diary and answer the questions.**

1 When was the party?
2 Where was it?
3 Who was there?
4 Who wasn't there?
5 Who was angry?

### Remember

2 years ago ← yesterday ← today<br>                 last night ← tonight<br>2 years ago ← last year ← this year

## Pronunciation – Weak and strong forms

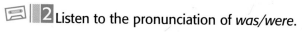

**2 Listen to the pronunciation of *was/were*.**

**Weak**    1 Where were you?    2 I was there.
**Strong** 1 He wasn't there.    2 We were!

**3 Listen and write S (strong) or W (weak). Then listen again and repeat.**

1 When were you born? (W)
2 I was angry.
3 Tom wasn't there.
4 Yes, he was!
5 Where were you on Monday?
6 Mickey was at Isabel's party.
7 We weren't there.

**4 Complete the conversation with the correct form of *was/were*. Then listen and check.**

**Mel** Tom! Where ¹ *were* you on Saturday? You weren't at Isabel's party!
**Tom** No, sorry. ² ... it good?
**Mel** Yes, it ³ ... . We ⁴ ... all there. Mickey and Isabel ⁵ ... worried. Where ⁶ ... you?
**Tom** Umm, Merlin ⁷ ... ill.
**Mel** Really? But you ⁸ ...n't at home.
**Tom** Actually, Merlin ⁹ ...n't really ill. I ¹⁰ ...n't at the party because Isabel is Mickey's girlfriend now.
**Mel** Oh Tom, she isn't. She likes Mickey but she likes you too.
**Tom** Oh. ¹¹ ... I wrong then?
**Mel** Yes, you ¹² ... ! Let's go and have a cola.

**5 In pairs, ask and answer about these times. Where was your partner?**

- on Monday morning
- on Tuesday evening
- three hours ago
- last night
- two days ago

A: Where were you on Monday morning?
B: I was at home/at the café.

*Natalie McIntyre, 1970...*

# FOCUS 3    Communication – Talk about the past

## Vocabulary – Years

**1** Listen and repeat.

a) 1836   c) 1991   e) 1989   g) 1901
b) 2000   d) 1976   f) 1942   h) 2010

**2** Ask three people in your class.

A: When were you born?
B: I was born in … (year).
A: When was your dad/sister born?
B: I think he/she was born in … .

Remember

nineteen forty

in nineteen forty

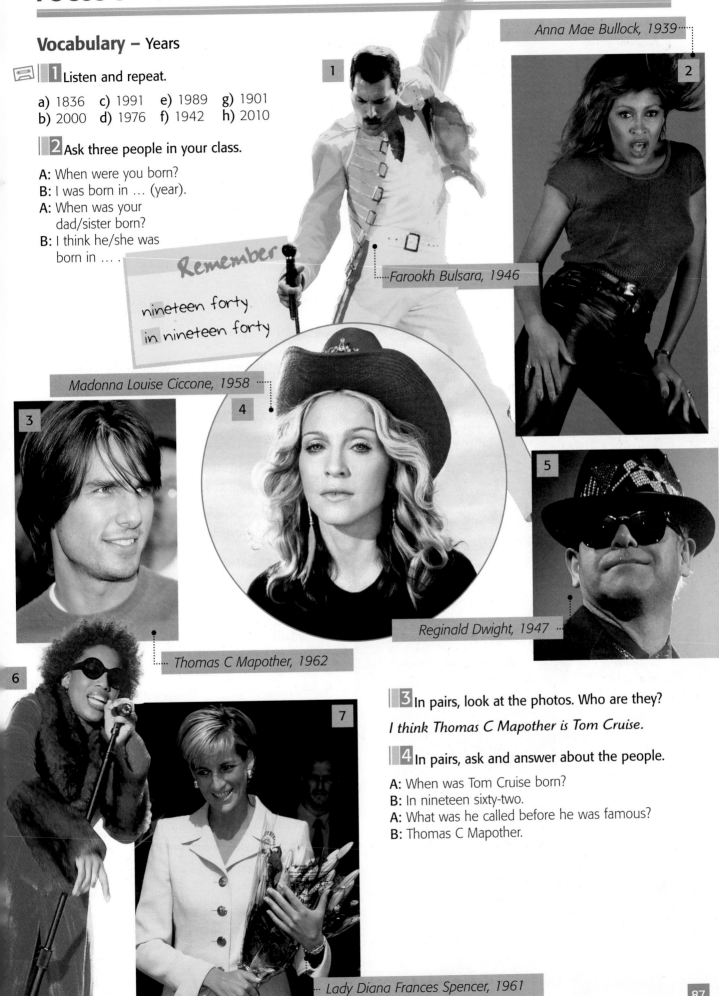

Anna Mae Bullock, 1939

Farookh Bulsara, 1946

Madonna Louise Ciccone, 1958

Reginald Dwight, 1947

Thomas C Mapother, 1962

Lady Diana Frances Spencer, 1961

**3** In pairs, look at the photos. Who are they?

*I think Thomas C Mapother is Tom Cruise.*

**4** In pairs, ask and answer about the people.

A: When was Tom Cruise born?
B: In nineteen sixty-two.
A: What was he called before he was famous?
B: Thomas C Mapother.

87

# FOCUS 4   Grammar – Past simple positive

| Regular verbs | | | | Irregular verbs | | | |
|---|---|---|---|---|---|---|---|
| I/you<br>he/she/it<br>we/they | } | lived<br>moved | started<br>stayed | I/you<br>he/she/it<br>we/they | } | went<br>came | got<br>met |
| *He lived in Los Angeles in 1998.* | | | | *He went to Los Angeles in 1988.* | | | |

### Think about language

**Make a rule.**
• Regular past tense verbs end in ... .

**1** Match the verbs with their irregular past tense forms.

| see   give   buy |
| win   have |
| make   become |

| gave   saw   made |
| won   had |
| became   bought |

**2** Read and answer the question. What is Elijah Wood's nickname?

# Elijah Wood

*Elijah Wood was born in Iowa in the USA on 28th January 1981. He became a child model when he was five. He went with his family to Los Angeles in 1988 and he acted in his first film, Back to the Future Part II, in 1989.*

*Elijah was a very good child actor – he had energy and a fantastic smile. He got lots of work – from 1989 to 2001 he made twenty-three films! Then, in 2001, he got the part of Frodo in The Lord of the Rings and he became a star.*

*In 1993 Elijah worked in TV. He was in Frasier and Homicide: Life on the Street.*

*He lives in Los Angeles now and he's got two pet dogs. His nickname is 'Monkey'.*

**3** Match the years to the correct information.

| 1 in 1981 | a) he/become/<br>a child model |
| 2 in 1986 | b) he was in *Frasier* |
| 3 in 1988 | c) Elijah Wood/be/born |
| 4 in 1989 | d) he/become/a star |
| 5 from 1989 to 2001 | e) he and his family/<br>go/to Los Angeles |
| 6 in 1993 | f) he/act/in his first film |
| 7 in 2001 | g) he/make/23 films |

**4** Write sentences from exercise 3 about Elijah Wood.

*1 Elijah Wood was born in 1981.*

**5** Write 6 past simple sentences about your life. Then tell your partner.

1  be born     *I was born ...*
2  start school in
3  my father/mother work
4  finish/primary school
5  go to my new school
6  live

### Memory Tip 8

**Surprise yourself.**
• Put new words in unusual places (your bathroom, your kitchen) to remember them.
• Write irregular verbs on notes.

# FOCUS 5  Vocabulary – Ordinal numbers and months

**1** Look at the list of ordinal numbers. Which colour is irregular?

| | | | |
|---|---|---|---|
| 1st | first | 14th | fourteenth |
| 2nd | second | 15th | fifteenth |
| 3rd | third | 16th | sixteenth |
| 4th | fourth | 17th | seventeenth |
| 5th | fifth | 18th | eighteenth |
| 6th | sixth | 19th | nineteenth |
| 7th | seventh | 20th | twentieth |
| 8th | eighth | 21st | twenty-first |
| 9th | ninth | 22nd | twenty-second |
| 10th | tenth | 23rd | twenty-third |
| 11th | eleventh | 24th | twenty-fourth |
| 12th | twelfth | 25th | twenty-fifth |
| 13th | thirteenth | | |

**2** Listen and say the numbers. Then write the numbers as words.

1st   2nd   3rd   10th   16th   24th   30th

*first, …*

**3** Put the months into the correct order. Then listen, check and repeat.

| | | | |
|---|---|---|---|
| April | August | December | February |
| January | July | June | March | May |
| November | October | September | |

*January, …*

**4** Say the dates.

1st January 2000    5th July 1954
18th November 1928    30th April 1789
20th July 1969    14th April 1912

*The first of January two thousand.*

## Find out!

**5** In pairs, match the dates in exercise 4 to the correct events in the pictures.

*Elvis Presley made his first record on … .*

**6** Student A check the answers on page 135. Student B check the answers on page 136.

A: What happened on the first of January two thousand?
B: …

**Memory Gym 13**

Dates and months

Go to page 122

# What happened when?

*Elvis Presley made his first record.*

*The first man walked on the moon.*

*The 21st century started.*

*Mickey Mouse starred in his first cartoon.*

*The Titanic started her first (and last) trip.*

*George Washington became the first president of the USA.*

# FOCUS 6   Skills – Meet Aimee Mullins

## Reading

**1** Check these words.

amputate   wheelchair   medal   fashion
designer   actress   strength   beauty

**2** Before you read look at the title and picture.
Then answer the questions.

1   What do you think the text is about?
2   What is different about this woman?

**3** Quick Read. Read and check your answers
to exercise 2.

### Study skills – Dictionaries

**Think before you use a dictionary**
- **E**xamine the word (is it a noun, verb or
  adjective?)
- **G**uess what it means in context.
- **G**o to the dictionary to check the meaning.

**4** Use EGG to check these words in the text.

1   disabled          2   operation

**5** Detailed Read. Read and answer true or
false. Correct the false sentences.

1   Aimee had an operation when she was two. ✗

*Aimee had an operation when she was one.*

2   She wanted a wheelchair.
3   She can't swim or play football.
4   Aimee was happy in her teenage years.
5   The 1996 Paralympic Games were in London.
6   She won one medal.
7   Alexander McQueen is a fashion designer.
8   Aimee became a model after the fashion show.

# Disabled?

## Nothing is impossible for Aimee Mullins.

When Aimee Mullins was born on 20th July 1975, there was a problem with her feet. At the age of one, she had an operation. Doctors amputated her feet and part of her legs. Aimee didn't want a wheelchair. She wanted to move around more, so she learned to walk when she was two. After that, Aimee learned to run, swim and play football.

Life at school wasn't always easy, but she enjoyed her teenage years. She played sports and she was a happy girl. As she became older, she became more confident.

Aimee can do a lot of different things. She is a fantastic athlete. In August 1996 she went to the Atlanta Paralympic Games in the USA, and won three medals. In 1999, she starred in a London fashion show for clothes designer Alexander McQueen. After that, she became a model. Aimee is now a TV and film actress too.

'There is no perfect body' Aimee says. 'My body isn't perfect, but I can be beautiful. My body helped me find my own strength and beauty.'

## Listening

**6** Listen to Katie talking about 5 important dates in her life. Write the dates. Listen again and write what happened on each date.

| Date | What happened? |
|---|---|
| 1 *2nd October 1990* | *She was born* |
| 2 | |
| 3 | |
| 4 | |
| 5 | |

## Speaking

**7** In pairs, check the information from exercise 6 about Katie.

A: She was born in  *1992* .
B: Yes./No, I think she was born in … .

**8** Think about your life. Write the dates of 5 important events.

*May 1982, 22nd June 1993, 2003, …*

**9** Show your partner the dates. Ask and answer about your dates.

A: What happened in May, nineteen eighty-two?
B: My parents met.

## Writing Gym 8

A webpage

Go to page 131

# Energy Check

## Grammar

**1** Complete with *was, were, wasn't* or *weren't*.

Mark  **1** _Were_ you at work yesterday?
Greg  No, I **2** … .
Mark  **3** … you at home?
Greg  Yes, I **4** … .
Mark  **5** … your parents at home?
Greg  No, they **6** …, but my grandparents **7** … there.
Mark  **8** … you ill?
Greg  No, I **9** …, but my dog **10** … . She's OK now.

**2** Put the questions into the correct order. Then answer the questions about you.

1  were/you/where/born/?

*Where were you born?*
*I was born …*

2  born/mother/was/your/when/?
3  first school/was/your/called/what/?
4  your/favourite/was/who/teacher/ at that school/?
5  who/best friends/were/at that school/your/?

**3** Complete the text with the correct form of the past simple.

We **1** (come) _came_ to Britain in 2001 and **2** (stay) … in London. I **3** (like) … it. We **4** (live) … in a little house and my brother **5** (work) … in a café. I **6** (go) … to school and **7** (help) … my brother in the evening. In 2002 my uncle **8** (give) … some money to the family and we **9** (move) … to a big house. We **10** (be) … very happy.

## Vocabulary

**4** Write the days, then put them into the correct order.

1  asunyd *Sunday*
2  dafiry
3  yddwenesa
4  yamond
5  draustay
6  dryutsah
7  stuyeda

*Sunday, …*

**5** Write the dates in full.

1  31/1/1995

*the thirty-first of January, nineteen ninety-five*

2  23/12/1902
3  8/8/1843
4  9/2/2008
5  12/7/1999
6  20/9/2010
7  15/4/2099

**6** Complete with the correct prepositions.

1  *on* Saturday
2  … nineteen twenty-five
3  … January
4  … half past three
5  … the twenty-fourth of November

## Communication

**7** Use the information to complete the conversation with Hanna about her life.

1990  I was born
1996  first school
1997  sister (Emma) born
2000  family moved to Italy
2001  started new school
2003  met Fulvio (boyfriend)

You    What happened in 1990?
Hanna  I was born.
You    …

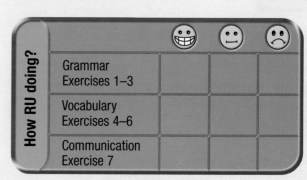

# Return to Sender

I gave a letter to the postman,
He put it in his sack.
Bright and early next morning
He brought my letter back.

She wrote upon it
'Return to sender, address unknown
No such number, no such zone.'

We had a quarrel, a lover's spat,
I write 'I'm sorry' but my letter keeps coming back.

So when I dropped it in the mailbox,
I sent it Special D.
Bright and early next morning,
It came right back to me.

She wrote upon it,
'Return to sender, address unknown
No such number, no such zone.'

This time I'm gonna take it myself
And put it right in her hand.
And if it comes back, the very next day
Then I'll understand the writing on it.

Return to sender, address unknown
No such number, no such zone
Return to sender …
Return to sender …

a spat = an argument

In 1953 a young man walked into the Sun Record Studios in Memphis Tennessee, USA. It was his lunch hour from the factory. He recorded two songs – a birthday present for his mother.

Who was that young man?
Elvis Aaron Presley was his name. He was nineteen. By 1956 he was an international star. He recorded *Return to Sender* in 1959. Rock 'n' Roll was teenage music and lots of parents hated it. He sold a billion records (that's 1,000,000,000!) and starred in thirty-three films. He died on the 16th August 1977.

**1** Before you listen, look at the title. What do you think the song is about?

**2** Listen. Who did he write the letter to?

a) his mum b) his girlfriend c) his sister

**3** Check these words.

postman   sack   quarrel   mailbox

**4** Which description tells the story in the song, A or B?

**A** He had a quarrel with his girlfriend. He wrote a letter to say, 'Sorry'. He gave the letter to the postman, but the postman gave it back. The address was wrong.

**B** He had a quarrel with his girlfriend. He wrote a letter to say, 'Sorry'. She sent the letter back. The address was correct but she didn't want to see him again.

93

# I love sport!

**Grammar**

*like* + verb + *-ing*
Past simple
  negative/questions

**Vocabulary**

Sport

**Communication**

Offer help
Talk about sport

**FOCUS 1**   Switch on

## Listening

**1** Check these words.

skateboard  trick  social committee
school hall  need  gig

**2** Listen and answer the questions.

1  Who does Mel speak to on her mobile?
2  What does he want?

## Reading

| Mickey | Hey, watch this! |
|---|---|
| Isabel | What's he doing? |
| Dave | He's doing a new skateboard trick. I think it's called a 'kick turn'. He learned it yesterday. |
| Mickey | Are you watching? |
| Tom | Yeah … we're watching. I hate skateboarding! |
| Isabel | Mel, that's your mobile. |
| Mel | Hello? Hi, Danny … yeah … wow! That's great! Yeah, OK. Bye! Woohoo! Listen! That was Danny Morrison on the phone. |
| Isabel | Who's Danny Morrison? |
| Mel | He's on the school social committee. |
| Tom | What did he want? |
| Mel | He wants NRG to play at a gig. |
| Tom | When? |
| Mel | Next Saturday in the school hall. |
| Dave | Fantastic! |
| Isabel | We need to make a poster. |
| Mel | Good idea. I can do that – I can use my computer. |
| Mickey | Did you see that? |
| Tom | No, we didn't. |
| Isabel | Sorry, Mickey. |
| Mickey | What? You didn't watch! I can't believe it! |

**3** Read and answer the questions.

1 What is Mickey's new trick called?
2 Does Tom like skateboarding?
3 Who's Danny Morrison?
4 When is the gig?
5 Where is the gig?
6 Is Dave happy about the gig?
7 Who can make a poster?
8 Is Mickey angry they didn't watch?

CU THERE !

NRG GIG

School Hall   Saturday 7.30pm

## Listening

**4** Listen to the conversation. Who does what? Tick (✓) the correct names for each activity.

| Things to do | Mel | Isabel | Tom | Mickey | Dave |
|---|---|---|---|---|---|
| 1 make a poster for the gig | ✓ | ✓ | | | |
| 2 talk to the social committee | | | | | |
| 3 tell the school newspaper | | | | | |
| 4 check the equipment | | | | | |
| 5 check the school hall | | | | | |
| 6 write an article about the gig for Mel's webpage | | | | | |
| 7 text our friends about the gig | | | | | |

## Roleplay – Offer help

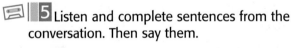

**5** Listen and complete sentences from the conversation. Then say them.

1 Isabel   _Let_ me do that.
2 Mel      Thanks, Isabel … I help you?
3 Dave     Oh, come on Mel. I … do that.
4 Isabel   I … do that.
5 Dave     Mel, …… check the equipment.
6 Mel      … you … help?

**6** You want to organise a disco at your school. Work in groups of 4 or 5. Who does what? Find one person for each task.

- talk to the head teacher
- make a poster
- check the equipment
- choose the music
- check the school hall

**1** Which sports in the box are in the photos?

| football   basketball   volleyball   baseball |
| tennis   swimming   running   ice hockey |
| cycling   skiing   gymnastics   surfing |
| skateboarding   snowboarding   Tae Kwon Do |

**2** Answer the questions.

1 Which sports are team sports?   *football, …*
2 Which sports do you play outside?
3 Which sports do you play with a ball?
4 What's your favourite sport?

**Remember**

play a game (play football)
but
go swimming
do gymnastics

**Memory Gym 14**

Sports

Go to page 122 ▶▶▶

## Grammar

**like + verb + -ing**

*I **like playing** tennis.*
*I **don't like watching** football.*
*I **love swimming**.*
*I **hate doing** gymnastics.*

**3** In groups, ask and answer the questions. Make notes about the sports people play or watch.

1  Do you like playing (football)?

A: Do you like playing football?
B: Yes, I do./No, I don't.

2  Do you like watching (football)?
3  Are you in a team?
4  How often do you play?
5  What's your favourite sport on TV?

## Writing

**4** In groups, collect information from the other groups. Draw a graph or write a report about your class.

*In our class, fifteen people play football …*

Number of students

97

# FOCUS 3 Grammar – Past simple negative/questions

| Negative | Questions | Short answers |
|---|---|---|
| I/you he/she/it we/they } didn't watch | Did { I/you he/she/it we/they } watch? | Yes, I did./No, I didn't. Yes, you did./No, you didn't. |
| *You didn't watch!* | *Did you see that?* | **Wh- questions** *What did he want?* *When did skateboarding start?* |

## THE HISTORY OF SKATEBOARDING

**When did skateboarding start?**

In 1958. Mark Richards and his dad Bill had a surf shop in California, USA. One day, they made a skateboard. They used a piece of wood and some old roller skates. Lots of surfers bought the skateboards and a new sport was born.

**When did skateboarding become popular?**

In 1965. The sport was only seven years old, but Americans bought thirty million skateboards.

**Where did people practise?**

The first skateboarders didn't have a special place to practise — they used empty swimming pools.

**Did skateboards change over the years?**

Yes, they did. The first skateboards didn't go very fast but in 1973, Frank Nasworthy invented the plastic wheel. The new skateboards were really fast!

**Did everyone like skateboarding?**

No, they didn't. In Norway, the government didn't like skateboarding — in 1980 they banned the sport!

**What's an 'Ollie'?**

Alan Ollie Gelfand invented a cool new trick in 1977 — he jumped! Now a skateboard jump is called an Ollie.

### Think about language

**Make rules.**
- To make a Past simple **negative** use ... + verb.
- To make a Past simple **question** use ... + verb.

**1** Make questions.

1 Where/Mark and Bill Richards/live/?

*Where did Mark and Bill Richards live?*

2 When/they/make/the first skateboard/?
3 What/they/use/?
4 How many skateboards/Americans/buy/ in 1965/?
5 Why/skateboarders/use/empty swimming pools/?
6 When/Frank Nasworthy/invent/the plastic wheel/?
7 When/Norway/ban/skateboarding/?
8 What/Alan Gelfand/invent/?

**2** Read the text and find the answers to the questions in exercise 1.

*1 They lived in California, USA.*

**3** Correct the sentences. Write true sentences.

1 The Richards had a music shop.

*They didn't have a music shop.*
*They had a surf shop.*

2 They made the first skateboard in 1988.
3 Surfing became popular in 1965.
4 Frank Nasworthy invented the skateboard.
5 The USA banned skateboarding.
6 Ollie Gelfand invented the skateboard.

# FOCUS 4   Communication – Talk about sport

## Find out!

 Do this quiz in 2 teams. Team A ask Team B their questions. Team B ask Team A their questions. Then ask your teacher for the answers.

A: Where did football come from – Brazil, Italy, Britain or China?
B: It came from … .

## Pronunciation – /eɪ/, /əʊ/, /aɪ/

 **2** Listen and repeat.

1 /eɪ/ hate  baseball  skateboard
2 /əʊ/ snowboard  go  nose
3 /aɪ/ like  cycling  ice hockey

**3** Listen and put the words into the correct columns.

| great | nine | smoke | white |
|-------|------|-------|-------|
| Oh | smile | make | Spain | no |

| /eɪ/ | /aɪ/ | /əʊ/ |
|-------|------|------|
| great | nine | smoke |

## Memory Tip 9

**Test yourself often!**

- Write a verb list in two columns. Write the infinitive in the left column and the Past simple in the right column.

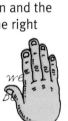

  go
  begin

- Cover one column and test yourself.

## Memory Gym 15

Irregular verbs

Go to page 123 ▷▷▷▷

## Sports Quiz!

### Questions for Team A

**1** Where did football come from?

A Brazil  B Italy  C Britain  D China

**2** When did people play the first game of tennis?

A 1,000 years ago  C 200 years ago
B 500 years ago  D 100 years ago

**3** Where did the Olympic Games start?

A France  C Great Britain
B Japan  D Greece

**4** Which country did Pelé play football for?

A Argentina  C France
B Britain  D Brazil

**5** What sport did Babe Ruth play?

A baseball  C football
B basketball  D volleyball

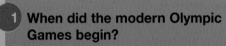

### Questions for Team B

**1** When did the modern Olympic Games begin?

A 1986  B 1964  C 1926  D 1896

**2** Which sport did Michael Jordan play?

A volleyball  C baseball
B basketball  D football

**3** Who won 16 Wimbledon tennis championships?

A Martina Martin  C Martina Navratilova
B Martina Tereschko  D Martina Smith

**4** Which team won the first football World Cup?

A Brazil  C Japan
B Italy  D Uruguay

**5** When was the first marathon?

A 7 years ago  C 2,500 years ago
B 22 years ago  D 200 years ago

 99

# David Beckham

When he was a child he wanted to play football. He didn't want to do other things. At school he was good at swimming and basketball but football was always his favourite sport. His parents helped him. They bought him a football and a new Manchester United kit every year. Manchester United was always his favourite team.

His dad played football and David always went to games with him. After every game, he practised with his dad. After school he went to the local park and stayed there until eleven o'clock at night. He practised a lot because he wanted to play for Manchester United.

Every summer from the age of thirteen he went to Manchester United for a training camp. When he was sixteen he left home. When he first arrived at Manchester United he felt very nervous because all his heroes were in the team.

His first game in the team was in September 1992. He was seventeen. His mum and dad were really surprised when he came on the pitch!

The first time David met Victoria Adams was after a football game in London. He only said 'hi' because he was shy. Victoria was very confident – she said 'hello' and they started talking. At home he wrote her phone number on six or seven pieces of paper. He didn't want to lose it! Victoria and David got married in Ireland on 4th July 1999. He cried when Victoria arrived because she looked really fantastic. His first son Brooklyn was born in March 1999 and Romeo was born in September 2002. Victoria and his children are his first team.

In July 2003, the family went to live in Spain and David left Manchester United to play for Real Madrid. They paid £25 million for him. He was very sad to leave Manchester United, but he liked his new life in Spain.

# FOCUS 5  Skills – A profile of David Beckham

## Reading

**1** Before you read, look at the text and answer the questions.

1  Where is the text from?
2  What is it about?
3  What do you know about the man?

**2** Check these verbs and find their past simple forms.

| leave | feel | say |
| --- | --- | --- |
| get married | cry | look |

*Remember*

Examine the word.
Guess the meaning.
Go to the dictionary.

**3** Quick Read. Check your answers to exercise 1.

**4** Find these words in the text and work out what they mean.

| kit | local | park | nervous |
| --- | --- | --- | --- |
| pitch | piece of paper | | |

**5** Detailed Read. Choose the correct answers.

1  David Beckham plays …
   a) football.   b) tennis.   c) volleyball.
2  His parents bought him … every year
   a) football tickets   b) a basketball
   c) a new kit
3  He always … Manchester United.
   a) liked   b) didn't like
4  He played his first game when he was …
   a) eleven.   b) sixteen.   c) seventeen.
5  When he first met Victoria she was …
   a) shy.   b) married.   c) confident.
6  He went to live in Spain in …
   a) 1999.   b) 2002.   c) 2003.

## Speaking

**6** Make notes about your sporting hero or a famous person you like. Think about these questions.

- What is his/her name?
- When did you start to like him/her?
- Why?
- Which sport does he/she do?
- *any extra information*

**7** Tell the class about your sporting hero.
*He/She's called … and he/she plays … for …*

## Listening

### Study skills –  Listening

**Listening for gist**
It's difficult to understand everything when you listen to people speaking English. Try to understand the main ideas.
- **Who** is speaking and **what** are they talking about?
- **Focus on what you understand** – don't worry about words you can't understand.

**8** Listen and answer the questions. Think about the study skill.

1  Who is talking?
2  What is he/she talking about?

**9** Listen again and answer the questions.

1  How old is Mary?
2  Where is she from?
3  Does she play in a football team?
4  When did she start playing football?
5  Who gave her the money for the camp?
6  At the camp, when did they play games?
7  Did she meet any famous players?

**Writing Gym 9**

A postcard

Go to page 132

# Energy Check

## Grammar

**1** Complete the sentences with the correct form of the past simple.

1 David Beckham (start) at Manchester United when he was sixteen.

*David Beckham started at Manchester United when he was sixteen.*

2 His parents (watch) him in his first game.
3 He always (like) Manchester United.
4 He (practise) football every night.
5 He (move) to Manchester.
6 He (meet) Victoria after a football match.
7 He (write) her telephone number on six pieces of paper.
8 They (go) to Ireland to get married.
9 He (feel) happy at the wedding.
10 They (become) very famous.

**2** Make past simple questions for the answers.

1 Mark Richards invented the skateboard.

**What *did Mark Richards invent*?**

2 No, she didn't. Mark and his dad invented it.
   **Did Mark's mum … ?**
3 He used wood and roller skates.
   **What … ?**
4 Frank Nasworthy invented a new wheel in 1973.
   **When … ?**
5 People practised in empty swimming pools.
   **Where … ?**
6 Norway banned skateboarding in 1980.
   **When … ?**
7 People learned new tricks.
   **What … ?**
8 No, he didn't. Alan Gelfand invented the Ollie.
   **Did Mark Richards … ?**

**3** Correct the sentences.

1 Pizza came from France. (✗ Italy)

*Pizza didn't come from France. It came from Italy.*

2 Harry Potter lived in Japan. (✗ Britain)
3 Pelé played baseball. (✗ football)
4 The Germans invented skateboarding.
   (✗ the Americans)
5 William Shakespeare came from Portugal.
   (✗ Britain)
6 The Olympic Games started in India.
   (✗ Greece)
7 The British invented the hamburger.
   (✗ the Germans)

## Vocabulary

**4** Look at the pictures. Lisa wrote what she likes (✓) and hates (✗). Write sentences for her.

*Lisa likes running. She hates playing tennis.*

**5** Write about which sports you like and hate from exercise 4.

*I like … . I hate … .*

## Communication

**6** Complete the conversation.

**Harry** We need to make a poster.
**Marie** I ¹ *can* do that.
**Harry** ² … you talk to the teacher?
**Anna** Yes, I ³ … .
**Felix** Sorry, I ⁴ … do that.

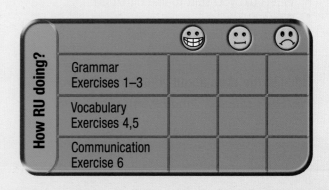

| How RU doing? | 😃 | 😐 | 😞 |
|---|---|---|---|
| Grammar Exercises 1–3 | | | |
| Vocabulary Exercises 4,5 | | | |
| Communication Exercise 6 | | | |

**2** I was always good at playing football because my brothers played with me in the garden at home. It's usually a boys' game but I didn't know that!

**3** I played in a girls' football team at school. The boys laughed when we played. Now they don't laugh because we often beat them!

**1** I'm Kerry and I'm fifteen. I come from Southampton. I love watching sport and I'm mad about football. I like other sports too – I'm a good runner and swimmer.

**4** I started playing with a real team – The Seagulls – when I was twelve. We train every Monday and Wednesday and we play a match on Saturday. We are third in the league at the moment. Which women's team do I support? Southampton of course!

*my team*

## Culture FILE

**In Britain**

- ✪ Only 40% of girls play sport or take exercise. 80% of boys do.
- ✪ Football is now the top female sport.
- ✪ In 1993 there were 80 girls' football teams. In 2003 there were 1,807.
- ✪ 62,000 women play for football teams.

## QUESTIONS

**1** Read about Kerry and answer true (T) or false (F).

1 She started playing football at school.
2 She trains twice a week.
3 Kerry supports Manchester United.
4 Only 80% of girls play sport.
5 Lots of women play football in Britain.

**2** In groups, discuss the questions.

1 Do girls and women play football in your country?
2 What sports do girls and women play?

MAD ABOUT = REALLY LOVE

# Projects

# Our Kind of Music

## Project 1 Our favourite band.

1. In pairs or groups, talk about your favourite bands. Each person chooses one band for the project.

2. Then each person finds...
   - a photo of their band
   - information about the life of one person in the band

3. In class, make a display. Use a big piece of paper and stick your photos on it.

4. Each person writes a short biography of a band member.

5. Attach the biographies to your display.

6. Think of a title and write it on the top of the display.

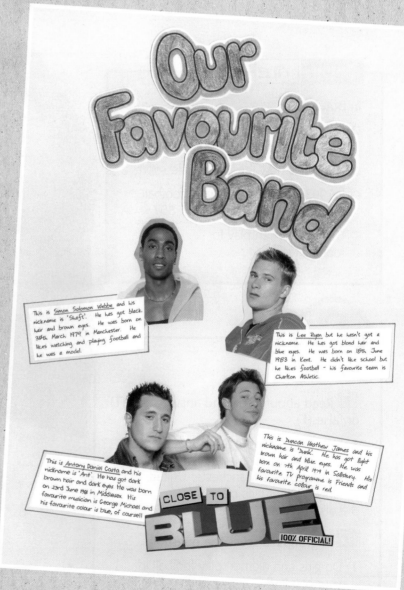

Our Favourite Band

This is Simon Solomon Webbe and his nickname is 'Shaft'. He has got black hair and brown eyes. He was born on 30th March 1979 in Manchester. He likes watching and playing football and he was a model.

This is Lee Ryan but he hasn't got a nickname. He has got blond hair and blue eyes. He was born on 18th June 1983 in Kent. He didn't like school but he likes football - his favourite team is Charlton Athletic.

This is Antony Daniel Costa and his nickname is 'Ant'. He has got dark brown hair and dark eyes. He was born on 23rd June 1981 in Middlesex. His favourite musician is George Michael and his favourite colour is blue, of course!

This is Duncan Mathew James and his nickname is 'Dunk'. He has got light brown hair and blue eyes. He was born on 7th April 1979 in Salisbury. His favourite TV programme is Friends and his favourite colour is red.

CLOSE TO BLUE
100% OFFICIAL!

# Project 2  Create a band.

**1** Invent the perfect band. First write the names of your band at the top of the poster.

**2** Draw a picture of the band or use photos from a magazine.

## JUICE

**4** Write part of one of their songs and a title.

### Juice it up!

We're Juice, what's up?
Where are you at?
Let's party, let's rock!
Come on and juice it up!

**3** Write a biography of the band. Think about the questions below.

Juice are a fantastic new rock band from Liverpool. Stu Watts (18) is the singer, Kim Jones (17) plays the guitar, Phil Gibson (19) plays the guitar too and his brother, Karl (20), is the drummer.

Stu and Kim were best friends at primary school. Later, they started a pop band together when they were thirteen. Three years ago, they left the band because they hated the music! They wanted to play rock, not pop.

Stu and Kim met Phil and Karl in the music room at college. Phil and Karl were great musicians and Kim was a great songwriter. With Stu's cool voice it was a perfect combination and Juice was born!

JUICE

Juice it up!

**5** Design a CD cover and draw it.

## Have some Juice now!

- What type of music do they play?
- How many people are in the band?
- What are their names and ages?
- What are their life stories?
- Where do they come from?
- Where did they go to school?
- Where did they learn to play music?
- What jobs did they do before?
- Where did they play their music?
- When and how did they meet?

**6** Write a message at the bottom of the poster.

# Congratulations – you're a band manager!

**Grammar**
*going to*

**Vocabulary**
Clothes

**Communication**
Ask permission

**FOCUS 1** Switch on

## Listening

**1** Check these words.

full   be sick   jeans   compliment
borrow   eyeliner   audience

**2** Listen and answer the question.

1   Who isn't on the stage?

## Reading

**Tom** Wow! Look at that! The hall's full.

**Mel** I can't believe it!

**Isabel** I'm nervous. I think I'm going to be sick.

**Dave** Urgghh, Isabel!!

**Isabel** I'm joking, Dave.

**Tom** Where's Mickey? He's late again.

**Dave** Hey, Isabel, I like your jeans. You look great.

**Isabel** Dave! That was a compliment! Are you all right?

**Dave** Yeah, ... can I borrow your eyeliner?

**Isabel** No, you can't! This isn't a metal band!

**Danny** OK. Let's start. You're going to be fantastic.

**Mel** Wait a minute, Danny. We haven't got a singer. Mickey's late.

**Dave** I'm going to kill him!

**Isabel** Relax, Dave! We don't want an argument now.

**Danny** It's OK. Mickey's talking to some girls in the audience.

**Isabel** What!? Now I'm going to kill him.

**Danny** OK, everyone. Welcome to the summer gig. Let's hear it for NRG!

### 3 Read the conversation and answer the questions.

1  Where is the band?
2  Mel says, 'I can't believe it!' Is she happy or sad?
3  Is Dave nice to Isabel?
4  What does he want to borrow?
5  Why can't the band start the concert?
6  Why is Isabel angry with Mickey?

### 4 Complete the phrases from the conversation. Then check what they mean.

1  Wow! _L o o k   a t_ that!
2  I can't b _ _ _ _ _ _ it!
3  You l _ _ _ great.
4  Wait a m _ _ _ _ _ .
5  R _ _ _ _ , Dave!

## Roleplay – Ask permission

### 5 Listen and complete the sentences from the conversation. Then practise saying it.

A: Can I ¹ _borrow_ a clean T-shirt?
B: Yes, sure. ² … you are.
A: Can I use your ³ …?
B: No, sorry you ⁴ … . I ⁵ … got one.

### 6 Student A think of things you want to borrow or use. Ask student B. Student B listen and answer.

borrow …
• a clean T-shirt      • your eyeliner
• five pounds          • your bag

use …
• your mobile          • your ruler
• your CD player       • your notebook

A: Can I borrow a clean T-shirt?
B: Yes, sure. Here you are.

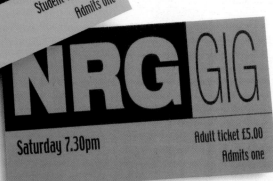

NRG GIG
Student ticket £3.50
Admits one
Saturday 7.30pm

NRG GIG
Saturday 7.30pm
Adult ticket £5.00
Admits one

# FOCUS 2  Vocabulary – Clothes

**1** Look at the photos below. What are people wearing? Use these words.

> shirt  T-shirt  jacket  boots
> trainers  sweatshirt  skirt  earring
> necklace  shoes  cap  trousers  jeans
> tie  gloves  helmet  shorts  suit

*He's wearing a red sweatshirt, blue jeans and trainers.*

**2** In pairs, talk about the clothes. Do you like them?

**A:** I like her jacket.
**B:** Yes, it's nice.
**A:** I don't like his suit.
**B:** No, it isn't cool, but I like him!

**3** In pairs, describe a person in your class. Who is it? Can your partner guess?

**A:** She's wearing red trousers and a yellow T-shirt
**B:** Is it Lena?

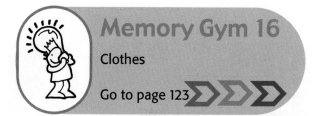

Memory Gym 16

Clothes

Go to page 123 ⟫⟫⟫

## Pronunciation – /e/, /ɜː/

**4** Listen and repeat.

/e/ r<u>e</u>d sw<u>ea</u>tshirt n<u>e</u>cklace
/ɜː/ sk<u>ir</u>t h<u>er</u> l<u>ear</u>n

**5** Listen and put the words into the correct columns.

> r<u>e</u>d  sk<u>ir</u>t  h<u>e</u>llo  p<u>er</u>son  g<u>ir</u>l
> g<u>e</u>t  n<u>e</u>xt  f<u>ir</u>st  m<u>e</u>n  p<u>er</u>fect

| /e/ | /ɜː/ |
|-----|------|
| *red* | *skirt* |

---

## Memory Tip 10

**Connect words in a wordweb.**

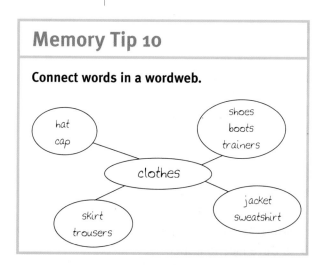

**6** Make a wordweb for the words in exercise 1. Add more words if you want to. Then show your partner. Are your wordwebs the same?

# FOCUS 3   Grammar – *going to*

| Positive | Negative | Questions | Short answers |
|---|---|---|---|
| I'm<br>You're<br>He's/She's/It's<br>We're/They're } going to start. | I'm not<br>You aren't<br>He/She/It isn't<br>We/They aren't } going to arrive. | Am I<br>Are you<br>Is he/she/it<br>Are we/Are they } going to see … ? | Yes, I am./No, I'm not.<br>Yes, he is./No, he isn't. |
| *We're going to start in five minutes.* | *Mickey isn't going to arrive at seven o'clock.* | *Are you going to meet him tomorrow?* | ***Wh-* questions**<br>*What time are you going to meet him?* |

### Think about language

**Make a rule.**

To make ***going to*** future use
***am/is/are*** + … + … .

Remember

five minutes ago ← now → in five minutes

yesterday ← today → tomorrow

**1** Match the people in the photos to the correct sentences. Then complete the sentences with the correct form of *going to*.

1 I (meet) *'m going to meet* my grandparents in South Africa tomorrow. They live in Cape Town.
2 I (meet) … some friends and we (play) … tennis.
3 I (race) … and I (win) … !
4 We (star) … in a rap video for TV. We (not be) … big, we (be) … megastars!!!
5 There's the bus! I (meet) … my mum. We (buy) … some new trainers.
6 I'm nervous. I (start) … my new job. I (not be) … late this morning!

**2** Listen, check and repeat.

**3** You won a competition. You and a friend can spend a day with your hero, anywhere in the world. Plan what you're going to do.

1 Who are you going to meet?
2 Who is going to go with you?
3 Where are you going to go?
4 What are you going to do …
   • in the morning?
   • in the afternoon?
   • in the evening?
5 What are you going to wear?

**4** In pairs, ask your partner about his/her day with his/her hero.

A: Who are you going to meet on Saturday?
B: I'm going to meet …

d

e

f

109

Eminem

Fred Durst

Britney Spears

Victoria Beckham

Robbie Williams

# What do your clothes say about YOU?

MUSIC IS BIG BUSINESS and image is very important to the stars. Stars know that clothes and make-up say a lot about their personality and their music. Some stars want an 'ordinary' image, so they wear ordinary clothes. American rock and rollers The Strokes wear casual jeans, shirts and T-shirts. Some stars change their image every year. Madonna has got a lot of different images. Clothes expert Maddy Thorn looks at the stars of today. What do their clothes say about them?

**A**

He's got different images because he sings different types of songs. He's wearing old-fashioned, smart clothes because he's going to sing an old-fashioned song.

**B**

Image is very important to her. She wears expensive clothes and lives in an expensive house. Some photographers from *Hi!* magazine are going to visit in an hour, so she's wearing smart clothes.

**C**

He's got prizes for music, but he still wears casual clothes on stage – a grey jacket and a black hat. He isn't going to change his image. He thinks music is the important thing.

**D**

She isn't working today – she isn't on stage. She's going to meet some friends in a café. She's wearing a T-shirt, jeans and sunglasses because today she's an ordinary person and she wants an ordinary life.

**E**

He's wearing strange clothes – gloves, no shirt and what has he got on his head?!

# FOCUS 4    Skills – It's all about image!

## Reading

**1** Check these words.

image    casual    change (v)
expensive    smart

**2** Quick Read. Read the text quickly.
Match the descriptions to the correct photos.

**3** Detailed Read. Read the text again and
answer the questions.

1  What type of clothes do The Strokes wear?

*Casual clothes*

2  Who has got a lot of different images?
3  Who doesn't have different images?
4  What type of song is Robbie going to sing?
5  What does Fred Durst think is important?
6  What is Britney wearing today?

## Listening

**4** Listen and write the names of 4 people in
the picture.

**5** Listen again and complete the table with
information about their clothes and personality.

| Name | Clothes | Personality |
|------|---------|-------------|
| *Paul* |  |  |
|  |  |  |
|  |  |  |
|  |  |  |

## Study skills – Speaking

**Conversational replies**    'Wow!'

When you have a conversation in English,
it's a good idea to show interest.

**6** Listen and complete. Use these words.

Mmm    You're joking    Why
I don't believe you    Really

1  **A:** I'm a student.
   **B:** *Mmm* ?
2  **A:** I study film and TV.
   **B:** … ?
3  **A:** I'm going to visit Hollywood this year.
   **B:** … ?
4  **A:** My mother's a film star.
   **B:** … !
5  **A:** She's going to get an Oscar.
   **B:** … !

**7** Listen again and repeat the replies.

## Speaking

**8** What are you going to do at the weekend?
Think about these questions and make notes.

1  Where are you going to go?
   *(a party; a disco; the cinema, a football game …)*
2  What are you going to do?
   *(dance, chat with friends, watch TV)*
3  What are you going to wear?
   *(a suit, a football shirt, a dress)*

**9** In pairs, ask and answer about your plans.
Use conversational replies.

**A:** What are you going to do at the weekend?
**B:** I'm going to … .
**A:** Really? What are you going to do there?

**10** Tell the class about your partner's plans.

*Elizabeth is going to …*

# FOCUS 5   The gig

## Reading

**Dave**     Listen to the audience!
**Isabel**   Wow! We're going to be famous.
**Mickey**  Mel! What did you think?
**Mel**      It was ... fantastic! The audience loved it.
             They loved you. You're a real band now!
**Danny**   Come on – they want more! What are you
             going to play?
**Dave**     We haven't got any more songs.
**Tom**      How about *Energy* again?
**Mickey**  Great idea.
**Isabel**   Everyone ready? Let's go!

**1** Read and listen. Then answer the questions.

1  What did the audience think
   of the band?
2  What did Mel think?
3  What are they going to
   do next?

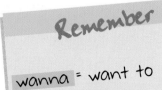

Remember

wanna = want to

**2** Listen and complete the song.

| spring | bright | sing | Monday |
|--------|--------|------|--------|
| night  | dreams | scream | |

### ENERGY!

I crawl out of bed on ¹ *Monday,*
My head full of ² ...
But the beat, beat, beat of energy
Makes me wanna ³ ... .

Charge me up, plug me in,
Switch me on, let's begin.

I fall out of bed in winter
I jump out of bed in ⁴ .........
And a beat, beat, beat of energy
Makes me want to ⁵ ... .

*Chorus*

Energy! Wakes me in the morning.
Energy! Middle of the ⁶ ... .
Energy! Buzzes right through me.
Energy! Burns so ⁷ ... .

## Dalesway News

ISSUE 7

JULY

# Big Bang – NRG

*By Danny Morrison*

NRG, our new school band, had their first concert on Saturday night. They played for two hours in the school hall and they were fantastic.

Mickey Kelly is the singer, Tom Adamski writes songs and plays guitar, Dave Black plays drums and the gorgeous Isabel Ferrante plays keyboards and sings. Mel Williams is the band manager. It's a great combination.

At eight o'clock on Saturday night the hall was full. No surprise, because Mel Williams put posters all over the school last week! Then NRG exploded onto the stage with a rocking version of *Sk8er Boi*. Mickey Kelly's got a superb voice. And the band? They aren't good – they're fantastic!!

By the end, the audience wanted more, more, more. NRG came back on stage to play *Energy!* Everyone agreed – this band has the energy to go all the way. Don't miss the next concert!

## Reading

**3** Read the review by Danny Morrison. Did he like the band?

**4** Answer the questions. Use Danny's review.

1 When was it?
2 Where was it?
3 What time did they start?
4 What did they play?
5 Did the audience like the band?
6 Did Danny like the band?

## Listening

**5** Listen to the end of the story. What happens to Isabel, Tom, Mel, Dave and Mickey?

## Writing Gym 10

A review

Go to page 133

*Is this the end or just the beginning .....?*

# Energy Check

## Grammar

**1** Make sentences with the correct form of *going to*.

1 I/travel in June

*I'm going to travel in June.*

2 my brother/not come
3 my brother and I/visit my grandparents
4 they/be in Paris
5 my parents/not visit them in June
6 we/have a great time!
7 I/come back in August
8 then I/study for my exams

**2** Make questions with *going to*.

1 what/you/do/tomorrow?

*What are you going to do tomorrow?*

2 Peter/play football too/?
3 is Kate/be there/?
4 what/we/play/?
5 I/see them tomorrow/?
6 you/see them/?
7 Mrs Green/talk to your parents/?
8 your parents/visit her/?

**3** Complete the letter with the correct form of *going to*.

Dear Max,

In July, we ¹ (go) *are going to go* to Italy.
My brother ² (visit) … friends in Rome, and I
³ (see) … to Venice. We ⁴ (not go) … to Milan.
My parents ⁵ (not come) … with us – they
⁶ (see) … my uncle in the USA. ⁷(be) … you …
in the USA in August? My mum and dad ⁸ (be) …
in Seattle, then they ⁹ (visit) … Washington. Where
¹⁰ (stay) … you … ? We ¹¹ (have) … a great time.
I really love Italy!

Love,

Lisa

## Vocabulary

**4** Describe the clothes.

## Communication

**5** Jess and Ally are going to go to a party.
Jess asks to borrow three things. Write the
conversation.

Jess    Can I borrow your ¹ *T-shirt* ?
Ally    ² *Yes, sure. Here you are* .
Jess    Can I borrow a ³ … ?
Ally    ⁴ … .
Jess    Can ⁵ … ?
Ally    ⁶ … .

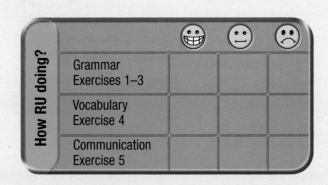

| How RU doing? | | 😁 | 😐 | 🙁 |
|---|---|---|---|---|
| | Grammar Exercises 1–3 | | | |
| | Vocabulary Exercise 4 | | | |
| | Communication Exercise 5 | | | |

# We're going to Ibiza

Hello party people!
This is Captain Kim speaking!
Welcome aboard Venga Airways
After take-off we'll pump up the sound system,
Because we're going to Ibiza!

I don't wanna be a bus driver
All my life.
I'm going to pack my bags and leave this town
Grab a flight.
Fly away on Venga Airways,
Fly me high
Ibiza sky.

Woah! We're going to Ibiza,
Woah! Back to the island.
Woah! We're gonna have a party,
Woah! In the Mediterranean Sea.

I oh I oh, oh we oh,
I oh I oh, oh we oh

Far away from this big town and the rain,
It's really very nice to be home again.
Fly away on Venga Airways
Fly me high, Ibiza sky.

*Chorus*

Thank you for flying Venga Airways.
We are now approaching Ibiza Airport,
As you can see the sky is blue
And the beach is waiting for you.

**vengaboys** are two men and two women, plus a cyber-friend called Cheekah. They come from Holland. Their first single was in 1997. They sold 10 million singles of the song and 5 million copies of their first CD.

*pump up = turn up*

This song is a 'cover' version – that means another band sang it first. 'Typically Tropical' sang it in 1975. The original song was called *We're Going to Barbados*. Vengaboys changed the underlined words.

1 Listen. Where are the people in the song?

2 Why are they happy?

3 They want to go to Ibiza. Where is your favourite holiday place?

4 Now it's your turn. Rewrite the song. Change the words which are <u>underlined in orange</u>.

115

# Memory Gym 1 – Countries and nationalities

* Use your memory – don't look back in the book.

* After each exercise go back and check. Revise words that you don't remember.

**1** **Remember.** Find the names of the countries.

**2** **Activate.** In pairs, take turns. Student A say a country. Student B say the nationality.

A: Japan
B: Japanese
A: How do you spell Japanese?
B: J-A-P-A-N-E-S-E

**3** **Remember.** Look at the pink boxes. What is the missing country?

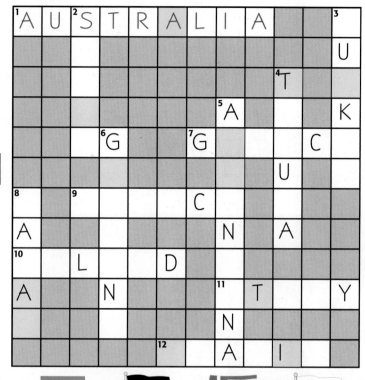

① ② ③ ④ ⑤ ⑥ ⑦ ⑧ ⑨ ⑩ ⑪ ⑫

# Memory Gym 2 – Everyday things

**1** **Remember.** Complete the crossword.

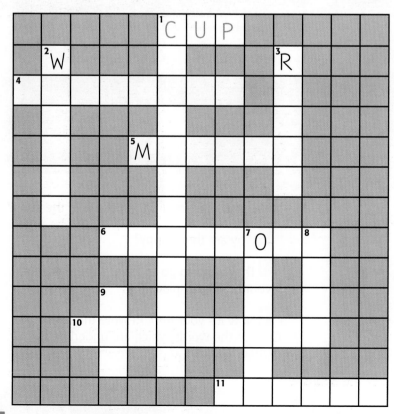

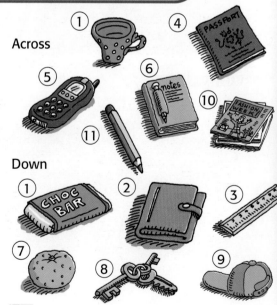

Across

① ④ ⑤ ⑥ ⑩ ⑪

Down

① ② ③ ⑦ ⑧ ⑨

**2** **Activate.** In pairs, tell your partner.

a) 5 food or drink words
b) 5 things for school

Now go to
WORDSTORE
p5 and 8

116

## Memory Gym 3 - Furniture and prepositions

**1 Remember.** Write the names of these things.

**2 Activate.** Say the furniture in your classroom. How many things can you name in English?

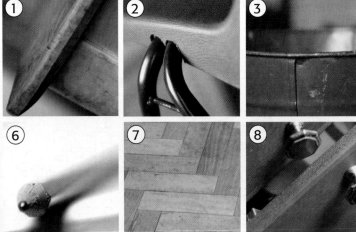

**3 Remember.** Write sentences. Where's Spot?

box

## Memory Gym 4 - Personality adjectives

**1 Remember.** Look at the pictures. Write the adjectives.

H _ _ _ _       S _ _       N _ _ _ _       F _ _ _ _ _ _ _

**2 Activate.** Now write the opposites.

*1 sad*
2
3
4

**3 Activate.** In pairs, A say an adjective. B say the opposite.

Now go to WORDSTORE
p9/10 and 13

# Memory Gym 5 – **Appearances**

**1** **Remember.** Match the words to the people in the pictures.

| fat | blond hair | beautiful | moustache | beard | slim | old |
|---|---|---|---|---|---|---|
| tall | short | bald | good-looking | curly hair | young | |

**2** **Activate.** Work in pairs. Student A describe someone from the picture. Student B guess who it is.

# Memory Gym 6 – **Families**

**1** **Remember.** In pairs, student A cover the words in the green box. Student B cover the words in the blue box. Then ask your partner to say the opposites.

**A:** father
**B:** mother

| mother | father |
|---|---|
| mum | dad |
| grandmother | grandfather |
| wife | husband |
| sister | brother |
| daughter | son |
| aunt | uncle |
| cousin | cousin |
| girlfriend | boyfriend |

**2** **Activate.** Describe your family. You are Mickey.

*Joe is my father, …*

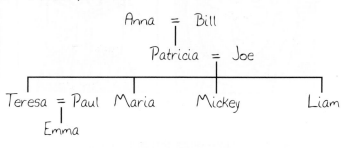

**3** **Activate.** Now do it again. You are Bill.

Now go to
WORDSTORE
p14 and 15

# Memory Gym 7 – Daily activity verbs

**Start**

07:00
06:30
08:30
08:00
6:45
05:30
06:30
09:00
09:00
11:30
7:00
09:30

**FINISH**

**1** **Remember.** Label each picture.

**2** **Remember.** In pairs or groups, take turns to say sentences about Rick's day.

✔ Correct words and grammar? Do the next picture then stop.

✘ Wrong words and grammar? Go back to the beginning and start again.

# Memory Gym 8 – Free time activities

**1** **Remember.** Match the verbs to the free time activities. You can use the verbs more than once.

swimming

homework          a book

your room              shopping

**read**

a friend      listen      go      friends

**watch   play**

football    **do**              to music

**meet    text**

TV

**tidy**              to a club

Tae Kwon Do

the piano

to the cinema

computer games

**2** **Activate.** Put the free time activities into a list. Number 1 is your favourite activity. Number 10 is the thing you hate!

1 _____
2 _____
3 _____
4 _____
5 _____
6 _____
7 _____
8 _____
9 _____
10 _____

**Now go to WORDSTORE p19 and 22**

# Memory Gym 9 – Rooms

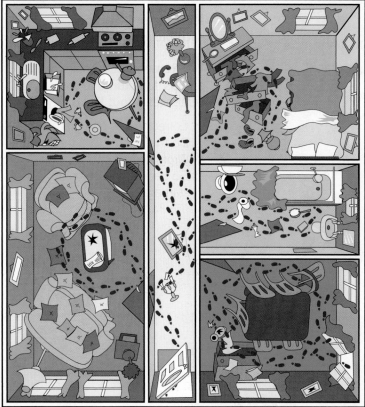

**1** **Remember.** Name the rooms.

1 A room with a bed in it.
2 You have lunch or dinner in this room.
3 There's a lot of water in this room.
4 You cook food in here.
5 I watch TV and relax in this room.
6 This long thin room has got a lot of doors!

**2** **Activate.** Follow the line through the house and say the names of the rooms (quickly!).

# Memory Gym 10 – Adjectives

**1** **Remember.** Find opposite adjectives.

| | |
|---|---|
| great | old-fashioned |
| interesting | dirty |
| modern | quiet |
| clean | terrible |
| loud | boring |

**2** **Activate.** What do you think of these things? Tell your partner.

| |
|---|
| rock music  English lessons  your classroom |
| your teacher's voice  computers  Abba |
| your bedroom  mornings  Backstreet Boys |

*I think rock music is great.*

**Now go to**
WORDSTORE
p23 and 26

## Memory Gym 11 – Parts of the body

**1 Remember.** Complete the words.

**2 Activate.** In pairs, student A say a word and student B point to the picture.

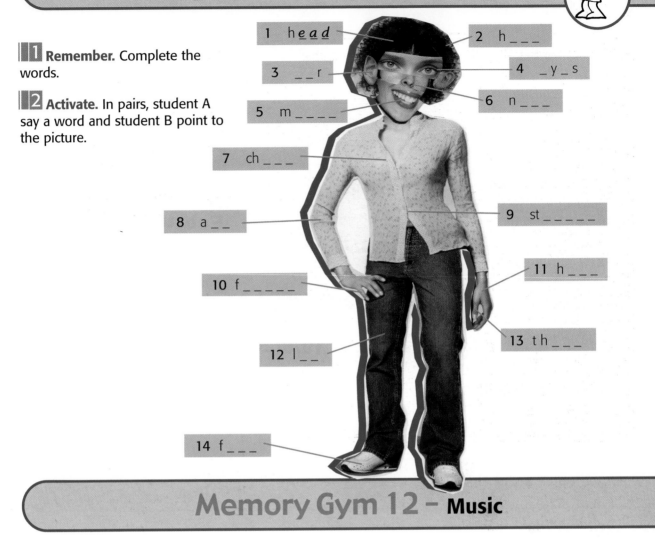

1 h e *a* *d*

2 h _ _ _

3 _ _ r

4 _ y _ s

5 m _ _ _ _

6 n _ _ _

7 ch _ _ _

9 st _ _ _ _ _

8 a _ _

11 h _ _ _

10 f _ _ _ _ _

13 t h _ _ _

12 l _ _

14 f _ _ _

## Memory Gym 12 – Music

**1 Remember.** Find 12 types of music in the grid. If you like, race another team.

| Z | F | U | Y | L | A | T | I | N |
|---|---|---|---|---|---|---|---|---|
| U | O | J | L | E | S | E | R | B |
| C | L | A | S | S | I | C | A | L |
| S | K | Z | N | O | P | H | P | U |
| L | E | Z | P | M | T | N | U | E |
| K | H | E | U | E | P | O | P | S |
| C | O | U | N | T | R | Y | J | Z |
| R | O | C | K | A | L | O | E | M |
| K | S | T | J | L | P | A | K | Y |

**2 Activate.** Write a list of music you like/don't like. Number 1 is your favourite music. Number 5 is music you hate.

1 _____
2 _____
3 _____
4 _____
5 _____

**Now go to WORDSTORE p27 and 30**

121

# Memory Gym 13 – Dates and months

**1 Remember.** Write the full names of the months.

1 J _ _ _ _ _ _ _
2 F _ _ _ _ _ _ _ _
3 M _ _ _ _ _
4 A _ _ _ _ _
5 M _ _
6 J _ _ _ _
7 J _ _ _
8 A _ _ _ _ _ _
9 S _ _ _ _ _ _ _ _ _
10 O _ _ _ _ _ _ _
11 N _ _ _ _ _ _ _ _
12 D _ _ _ _ _ _ _ _

**2 Activate.** Write the dates in full.

the 26th of February 2003

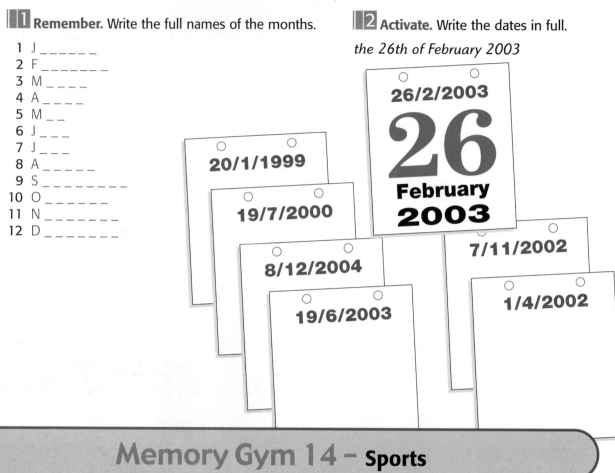

26/2/2003
**26**
**February**
**2003**

20/1/1999

19/7/2000

8/12/2004

19/6/2003

7/11/2002

1/4/2002

# Memory Gym 14 – Sports

**1 Remember.** Find the sports.

**2 Activate.** Put the sports into the correct groups.

A play *tennis* ......... ......... ......... .........

B do ........

C go ......... ......... ......... ........

Now go to
WORDSTORE
p33 and 36

## Memory Gym 15 – Irregular verbs

**1 Remember.** Which 6 past simple forms can you find? Write the missing forms.

> come   get   win   meet   buy
> give   become   go   make   have

**2 Activate.** In pairs, student A say a verb. Student B say the past simple form.

A: Come
B: Came

| B | O | U | G | H | T |
|---|---|---|---|---|---|
| E | G |   | W |   | A |
| C | A | M | E |   | D |
| A | V |   | N |   |   |
| M | E |   | T |   |   |
| E | M | E | T |   |   |

## Memory Gym 16 – Clothes

**1 Remember.** Find 13 items of clothing in the picture.

**2** Put the clothes into the correct groups.

**cool clothes** – I really like these clothes.
**uncool clothes** – I really don't like these clothes.
**OK** – these clothes are all right but they aren't special.

**3 Activate.** Complete the clothes wordweb.

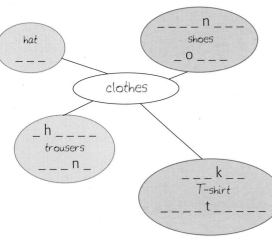

hat
_ _ _

clothes

_ _ _ _ n _ _ _
shoes
_ o _ _ _

_ h _ _ _ _
trousers
_ _ _ n _

_ _ _ k _ _
T-shirt
t
_ _ _ _ _ _ _

Now go to
WORDSTORE
p37 and 40

# Writing Gym 1 – An e-mail

**Writing Tip** – Capital letters

Use a capital letter …

a at the beginning of a sentence.
*She's a new student.*

b for names.
*Isabel Ferrante.*

c for countries, nationalities, towns, cities, streets, rivers.
*Argentina, Italian, Warsaw, Minster Street, the Amazon*

d for the word I.
*I'm American!*

e for songs, books and films.
*Gladiator, Lord of the Rings*

**1** Find the mistakes in Mel's e-mail and rewrite it correctly.

**From:**    Mel Williams
**To:**      John Jeffrey
**Subject:** e-pals

(hi) there,

my name is mel williams. i'm from manchester in britain. I'm british and I'm sixteen. my favourite singer is robbie williams. write to me!

best wishes,

mel

**2** Put this e-mail from Isabel into the correct order. Use Luisa's e-mail on page 16 to help you.

a) Isabel
b) Best wishes,
c) Please write to me!
d) My name's Isabel Ferrante. I'm from Argentina and my favourite animal is my cat, Ricky.
e) **From:**    Isabel Ferrante
   **To:** e-pals
f) Hi!
g) **Subject:**   I want an e-pal!

**3** Write a reply to Luisa's e-mail on page 16. Use this plan and Luisa's e-mail to help you. Make notes first. Then write a draft in your notebook.

## Plan

- Complete the To:, From: and Subject: boxes.
- Write a greeting.
  Hi, Luisa.
- Write about …
  your name/surname/nickname
  your town/country/nationality/age
  your favourite things/films/animals/
  places/colours
- Finish your e-mail.
  Please write …

**4** Check your draft. Check the capital letters in your e-mail. Write a good copy in your notebook.

# Writing Gym 2 – A letter about your room

**1** Use a plan of your bedroom and write about the position of the furniture. You are at the door. Add adjectives to your writing.

*There's an old brown cupboard on the left. There's a chair next to the desk.*

**2** Put the parts of the letter into the correct order. Use Robert's letter on page 26 to help you.

a) How are you? We are fine. We are in a new house. Our new address is at the top of this letter.

b) Dear Diana,

c) Best wishes,

d) Miguel

e) 17 Prospect Street
   Manchester
   England
   M21 5TV

**3** Write a letter to your friend about your room. Use Robert's letter on page 26 and this plan to help you. Make notes first. Then write a draft in your notebook.

## Plan

• Write about ...
   the size of your room.
   the position of the furniture.
   the age, size or colour of the furniture.
   the things on the walls.
   some of the things on the tables/shelves.
   your favourite thing(s) in the room.

**4** Check your draft. Check the adjectives in your letter. Write a good copy in your notebook.

# Writing Gym 3 – A description of a person

**Writing Tip** – Linkers *and/but*

**a** Connect ideas with *and* or *but*.

**b** Use *and* to connect positive ideas.
*She's tall and she's slim.*

**c** Use *but* to contrast ideas.
*He's intelligent but he isn't good at school.*

**1** Connect the sentences with *and* or *but*.

1  Leia's slim. She's beautiful.

*Leia's slim and beautiful.*

2  John's got black hair. He's got blue eyes.
3  She's friendly. She hasn't got many friends.
4  I'm tall. I've got long curly hair.
5  She's noisy. She isn't very confident.
6  Jackie is English. Her dad is Italian.

**2** Complete the description of Leia.

| and | is | her | but | is |
|-----|----|----|-----|----|

**LEIA**

Leia ¹ …    slim ² … she's got long dark hair.  She's 1.5 metres tall. ³ … brother is called Luke – she ⁴ … his twin sister.  She is confident ⁵ … quiet.

**3** Look at the information about Darth Vader and write a description of him. Connect your ideas with *and* or *but*.

**DARTH VADER**
**Appearance** very tall, has got a black mask
**Height** 1.85 metres
**Favourite colour** black
**Other:** very confident and unfriendly, hasn't got many friends

*Darth Vader is very confident and he's tall.*

**4** Write a description of two friends. Use the *Star Wars* descriptions on page 36 and this plan to help you. Make notes first. Then write a draft in your notebook.

## Plan

• Make notes about your friends.

What are their names?
What are their nicknames?
How old are they?
What do they look like?
What is/are their favourite thing(s)?
Other

**5** Check your draft. Check the grammar and linkers. Write a good copy in your notebook.

# Writing Gym 4 – A description of a daily routine

**1** Connect the sentences with *so* or *because*.

1 Eduardo goes home at the end of the week. His family are happy.

*Eduardo goes home at the end of the week, so his family are happy.*

2 The 'Chewing Gum Kit' helps the chicleros. It gives them work.
3 Suzanne's day isn't normal. She works at night.
4 I'm a taxi driver in London. I start work very early.
5 They finish work at nine o'clock in the evening. They are very tired.
6 I get up early. School starts at 7.30am.

**2** Complete the text about Suzanne's daily routine. Use linkers *and*, *but*, *so* or *because*.

Suzanne is from Britain ¹ *and* she lives in London with her husband. Suzanne is a doctor
² … she works hard. Her routine is strange
³ … she works at night. Suzanne gets up at six o'clock in the evening. She has dinner ⁴ … goes to work. She finishes work at half past six in the morning, ⁵ … she doesn't go home – she goes to the gym. Suzanne goes home at quarter past eight ⁶ … has breakfast at half past eight. She watches TV or reads. She goes to bed at eleven o'clock in the morning.

**3** Write a description about the daily routine of someone you know. Use the text about Eduardo on page 48 and this plan to help you. Make notes first. Then write a draft in your notebook.

## Plan

- Introduce the person and his/her family.
- Where is he/she from?
- If you want, explain the person's job.
- What does he/she do every day? (connect your ideas with and/but/so/because)
- Describe the person's daily routine.

**4** Check your draft. Check the linkers in your description. Write a good copy in your notebook.

## Writing Tip – Punctuation

**a** Use a capital letter to begin a sentence and a full stop to end it.
*There are twenty students in my class.*

**b** Use commas for lists.
*We play football, meet friends or do our homework.*

**c** Use a question mark at the end of a question.
*Do you do a lot of homework?*

**d** Use an exclamation mark at the end of a surprising sentence.
*Students clean the school after their lessons!*

**1** Rewrite the sentences with the correct punctuation.

1 there are thirty students in my class

*There are thirty students in my class.*

2 there are ten tables four windows twenty chairs and a door in my class
3 how many rooms are there in your school
4 do you go to school every day
5 we play football go to a café or talk to our friends after school
6 i don't do a lot of homework

**2** Read the description of Masahiro's school. Find 7 punctuation mistakes and correct them.

My school is small – it is in a town called Sakata There are 500 students from twelve to sixteen years old. i go to school at eight o'clock in the morning and I finish at three o'clock. we go to school six days a week. What do I like about school. I like football English and Kendo Club. Do I have a lot of homework? Yes, I go to homework school on Saturday? I like my school – but my favourite time is after school when I can chat with my friends

**3** Write an article about your school. Use the text on page 59 and this plan to help you. Make notes first. Then write a draft in your notebook.

## Plan

- Title
  What do you want to call your article?
- Introduction
  Give a general description of your school.
  Where is it?
  How many students are there?
  How old are they?
- Main report
  Write these three questions and answer them.
  When do you go to school?
  What do you do after school?
  Do you do a lot of homework?
- Conclusion
  Do you like your school? Why/Why not?

**4** Check your draft. Pay attention to the punctuation in your article. Write a good copy in your notebook.

## Writing Tip – Paragraphs

a When you plan your writing, organise your ideas into groups.

b Put each group of ideas into a paragraph so that each paragraph is about a different idea. Leave a space before each paragraph.

→ *My cat's called Chocolate because he's brown. He's got brown eyes too.*

**1** Put the text into 3 paragraphs.

Michael is Koko's friend. He's a gorilla. He lives in the USA. He's got black hair, brown eyes and a silver back. He likes music. Michael can use sign language. He can't speak but he can understand about 600 words. Michael can draw pictures too. Michael and Koko are part of the Gorilla Language Project. The project asks the question 'Can gorillas talk?' Dr Patterson is Koko's teacher but she works with Michael too. Michael is a very intelligent gorilla.

**2** Use the words to complete the information about Lucky.

> run   10   shoes   swim   eat a lot
> crisps   play football   short   dog
> brown   white   old bones
> sing (when he hears music on the radio)

| Name | *Lucky* |
|---|---|
| Type of animal | |
| Age | |
| Description | |
| What he likes | |
| What can he do? | *run* |

**3** Write a description of a special animal. Write about an animal you know or write about Lucky. Use the text about Koko on page 68 and this plan to help you.

## Plan

Paragraph 1 – Introduction
- name
- type of animal
- age
- a description
- What does the animal like?

Paragraph 2
- What can/can't this animal do?

Paragraph 3
- What do you think about this animal?

**4** Check your writing. Check the paragraphs in your description. Write a good copy in your notebook.

**Writing Tip** – Addresses and phone numbers

**a** Addresses

| | |
|---|---|
| Flat/House number + Street | 5, East Street |
| Town | Lincoln |
| Region | Lincolnshire |
| Postcode | MY4 2ER |
| Country | Great Britain |

**b** Telephone numbers

| | |
|---|---|
| international code | 0044 |
| area code | 0134 |
| local number | 678461 |

**1** Rewrite the address in the correct way.

I live in Brighton, in Great Britain. I live in Green Street. My house number is 8. Brighton is in Sussex. My Post code is BN4 5WV.

**2** Complete with the correct information about you.

Surname _____
First name _____
Age _____
Title (Mr/Mrs/Ms/Miss) _____
Address _____
Phone number  Area code _____
              Local number _____

**3** Ask your teacher for a *Pop Dreams* form and complete it. Use this completed form and the plan to help you.

## POP DREAMS    Entry form

Please write in CAPITAL LETTERS

Surname Y A T E S

First name D A V I D  Title M R

Address: Street 1 0  E A S T  S T R E E T

Town L I N C O L N  Postcode L 5 2 5 B X

Country G R E A T  B R I T A I N

Telephone 0 1 3 4  6 7 8 4 6 1

Date of birth (dd/mm/yy) 0 8 0 3 8 8

Sex (M/F) M

Nationality B R I T I S H

Favourite band or singer S H A K I R A

Favourite music or song P O P  M U S I C

Why do you want to enter Pop Dreams?

(maximum 60 words) I want to enter Pop Dreams because I want to be a pop star! I can sing, dance and play the piano. I've got a great voice and I can sing in front of lots of people. I'm confident and friendly and I think I'm good-looking (!) Choose me! I want to win!!

### Plan

- Why do you want to be on Pop Dreams?
- What can you do?
- Describe yourself.
- Finish your description.

**4** Check your form.

# Writing Gym 8 – A webpage

**1** Today is Saturday 11th June 2005. Rewrite these times using a different time phrase.

1 Friday 10th June 2005    *yesterday*
2 June 2004
3 May 2005
4 July 2004
5 Saturday 4th June 2005
6 your birthday
7 when you started school

**2** Complete the wordweb with information about you.

**3** Write a webpage about you. Use Tom's webpage on page 84 and this plan to help you. Then write a draft in your notebook.

## Plan

- Early History
  I was born in ... . My mother/father is a/an ... .
  I moved to ... when I was ... .
- Schools
  My first school was ... . I started there ... .
- Home life
  I usually/never help at home. On Tuesday afternoon I usually go to ...
- Interests
  I started [the piano] three years ago.

**4** Check your draft. Check the time phrases. Write a good copy in your notebook.

**My early history**

Born – where?
Parents (names/jobs)
Brothers and sisters
Home town
Other interesting information

**School**

Names of my schools
School now
Opinions about school
Favourite subjects

**ME**

**Home life**

Have you got a routine?
Do you help in the house?
What things do you do?

**Interests**

What can I do?

# Writing Gym 9 – A postcard

**Writing Tip –** Past Simple regular verbs spelling

Look at these spelling changes:

**a** help ➡ help**ed**
play ➡ play**ed**

**b** practise ➡ practis**ed**
try ➡ tri**ed**

**c** ban ➡ ban**ned**

**1** Read the writing tip. Rewrite this text in the past simple positive.

Hi Mum,

We ¹ (arrive) **arrived** here on Saturday. Yesterday we ² (start) … training at eight o'clock and ³ (stop) … at five. We ⁴ (play) … football. In the afternoon we ⁵ (try) … to play basketball. I wasn't very good at first but Suzie ⁶ (help) … me! I ⁷ (practise) … all day and now I can shoot a basket!

See you soon!

Mary

**2** Look at this postcard from Mary to her friend. Match the instructions to the correct numbers.

**a)** say hello
**b)** describe your holiday
**c)** say goodbye
**d)** write some extra information
**e)** write the date    *1*
**f)** write the address

**3** Write a postcard from a sports, music or film camp. Use this plan to help you. Make notes first. Then write a draft in your notebook.

Plan

- Say hello.
- Describe the camp.
- Say what happened on Saturday, Sunday and Monday.
- Describe what you liked doing.
- Say what you didn't like doing.
- Say hello from a friend.
- Say goodbye
- Add a 'P.S.'.

**4** Check your draft. Pay attention to spelling. Write a good copy on a real postcard.

1  Wednesday 5th August

2  Dear Matt,

3  Football Camp is fun. We arrived here on Saturday evening and played football. On Sunday we walked into Manchester and went to the cinema. In the evening we played computer games and I chatted to Emma on the Internet.
On Monday we practised and then watched football videos. In the evening we visited Old Trafford and I met David Beckham and Ryan Giggs!

4  See you soon!
Love
Mary

5  P.S. David Beckham and Ryan Giggs are very good-looking!

6  Matt Hooper
53 Lily Avenue
Preston
England
PR5 7CK

# Writing Gym 10 – A review

**Writing Tip – Strong adjectives**

a Use strong adjectives to make your writing more interesting.

*NRG were good.* ➡ *NRG were fantastic!*

*She's got a bad voice* ➡ *She's got a terrible voice!*

**1** Do these adjectives have a positive or negative meaning? Put them into the correct groups.

| fantastic | awful | great | terrible | superb |
|-----------|-------|-------|----------|--------|
| brilliant | rocking | cool | excellent | |

| good | bad |
|------|-----|
| fantastic | awful |

**2** Read this review of a rock concert. Replace the underlined adjectives with strong adjectives.

On Saturday evening last week, Martians played a concert in the new school hall in front of an audience of a hundred people. They played for two hours and they were <u>good</u>. Mark James is the singer and plays keyboards and Jennie Jones sings, plays the guitar and writes the <u>good</u> songs. The only problem is Jason Merry – he's the drummer and he's <u>bad</u>. He can't play in time!!

Martians played some original songs and some old songs. My favourite was *Blue* – it was <u>good</u>. I think Martians are going to be a <u>good</u> band because they've got some <u>good</u> songs and a lot of energy, but they need to find a new drummer!

**3** Write a review of a concert, film or play. Use Danny's review on page 113 and this plan to help you. Then write a draft in your notebook.

## Plan

- What was it called?
- When was it?
- Where was it?
- Describe the people?
  There were thirteen people on stage. They were called ...
- What happened?
  The band played ...
  The audience ...
- What did you think?
  It was fantastic and ...
  I hated it.
  It was terrible, because ...

**4** Check your draft. Pay attention to the strong adjectives in your review. Write a good copy in your notebook.

# Student B Information  Find out!

## Starter Page 8 – Exercise 2

In pairs, complete the chart. Student B look at this page, Student A look at page 8.

A: What's number one?
B: It's …
A: How do you spell it?

| | | |
|---|---|---|
| 1 | | *(handwritten)* |
| 2 | ▲ | **Beyonce** |
| 3 | NEW | **Busted** |
| 4 | | *The Cheeky Girls (handwritten)* |
| 5 | | |
| 6 | ▲ | **Elton John** |
| 7 | | |
| 8 | ▲ | **Robbie Williams** |
| 9 | ▼ | **Jennifer Lopez** |
| 10 | | *Madonna (handwritten)* |
| 11 | | *Christina Aguilera (handwritten)* |
| 12 | NEW | **Coldplay** |
| 13 | | |
| 14 | ▲ | **Dido** |
| 15 | ▼ | **The White Stripes** |
| 16 | | *Shakira (handwritten)* |
| 17 | ▼ | **Ashanti** |
| 18 | | *Eminem (handwritten)* |
| 19 | ▼ | **Ms Dynamite** |
| 20 | | *Sugababes (handwritten)* |

## Unit 1 Page 13 – Exercise 5

Student A

In pairs, use questions 2–7 from exercise 2. Who is your partner? Student A use the information on this page. Student B use the information on page 136.

A: Where are you from?
B: I'm from … .

| From: | Seattle, USA |
|---|---|
| Age: | (born 1955) |
| Father: | William Gates |
| Mother: | Mary Gates (teacher) |
| Favourite things: | computers, golf |
| Your name: | Bill Gates |

## Unit 2 Page 25 – Exercise 2

In pairs, student A look at the photo of Torin's classroom on page 25. Student B look at the photo of a British classroom on this page. There are differences in A's picture. What are they?

A: Are there books in your picture?
B: Yes, there are./ No, there aren't.
A: How many students are there?
B: Sixteen.

## Unit 3 Page 35 – Exercise 1

In pairs, complete Mel's family tree. Student B look at this family tree, Student A look at page 35. Ask questions to find the names of her family.

B: What's Mel's mother called?
A: Esther. What is her father called?

*Mel's Family Tree*

Etta = Marcus

Esther = Louis     Jan = Ronnie

Ann   Mel   Luke   Zak   Sarah

# Student B Information  Find out!

## Unit 4 Page 47 – Exercise 6

In pairs, complete the missing information.
Student B look at the information on this page.
Student A look at page 47.

**Friday** 19th July

**BBC1**

6.00 **Friends** The one where Ross meets a new girlfriend.
6.30 **The Simpsons**
6.50 **Top of the Pops** With Oasis and Dido.
7.30 **Football Focus**
8.30 **Film: The Beach** Starring Leonardo DiCaprio
11.45 **Night Music**

## Unit 5 Page 57 – Exercise 4

Complete the map of Isabel's house. Student B look at this page. Complete map A. Student A look at page 57.

A: Where is the bathroom?
B: It's next to …

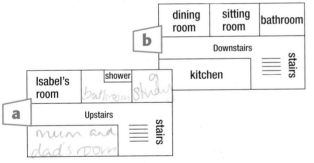

## Unit 6 Page 64 – Exercise 5

In pairs, talk about what Keanu Reeves can do. Student B look at this page. Student A look at page 64.

| Student B | |
| --- | --- |
| surf | ✓ |
| use a computer | ✓ |
| speak Spanish | ✓ |
| speak Japanese | ✗ |
| sing | ✓ |
| dance | ✓ |
| play the guitar | ✓ |
| run 1 kilometre | ✓ |
| swim | ✗ |
| write songs | ✓ |
| read music | ✓ |
| play the piano | ✓ |

## Unit 8 Page 89 – Exercise 6

Student A

In pairs, ask about the dates and check your guesses. Student A ask B about these dates:

5th July 1954
14th April 1912
1st January 2000

A: What happened on ………………?

**Then answer B about these dates:**

18th November 1928 – Mickey Mouse starred in his first cartoon.
20th July 1969 – The first man walked on the moon.
30th April 1789 – George Washington became the first president of the USA.

# Student B Information  Find out!

## Unit 7 Page 78 – Exercise 2

In pairs, student A you are the seller. Look at page 78. Student B look at this page. You are the buyer. Complete the prices of the things in the photo.

football shirts £23.00
posters £5.50
caps £....     3.99
dolls £12.50
bus £4.50
cameras £5.99
pencils 80p
postcards 80..p
pens £....
sunglasses £....     8.75
wallets £....     6.50
notebooks 75p     1.15

## Unit 1 Page 13 – Exercise 5

Student B

In pairs, use questions 2–7 from exercise 2. Who is your partner? Student B use information on this page. Student A use the information on page 134.

A: Where are you from?
B: I'm from … .

| From: | Louisiana, USA |
|---|---|
| Age: | (born 1981) |
| Father: | Jamie Spears |
| Mother: | Lynne Spears |
| Favourite things: | my dog, Cane |
| Your name: | Britney Spears |

## Unit 8 Page 89 – Exercise 6

Student B

In pairs, ask about the dates and check your guesses. Student B ask A about these dates:

18th November 1928
20th July 1969
30th April 1789

A: What happened on …

Then answer A about these dates:

5th July 1954 – Elvis Presley made his first record.
14th April 1912 – *The Titanic* started her first (and last) trip.
1st January 2000 – the 21st century started.